Who Defines Indigenous?

Who Defines Indigenous?

Identities, Development, Intellectuals, and the State in Northern Mexico

CARMEN MARTÍNEZ NOVO

RUTGERS UNIVERSITY PRESS

NEW BRUNSWICK, NEW JERSEY, AND LONDON

Library of Congress Cataloging-in-Publication Data

Martínez Novo, Carmen, 1966-
Who defines indigenous? : identities, development, intellectuals, and the state in northern
Mexico / Carmen Martínez Novo.
    p. cm.
  ISBN-13: 978-0-8135-3668-2 (hardcover : alk. paper)
  ISBN-13: 978-0-8135-3669-9 (pbk. : alk. paper)
  1. Mixtec Indians–Mexico–Tijuana (Baja California)–Ethnic identity. 2. Mixtec Indians–
Mexico–Tijuana (Baja California)–Social conditions. 3. Mixtec Indians–Mexico–Tijuana (Baja Cali-
fornia)–Economic conditions. 4. Indian business enterprises–Mexico–Tijuana (Baja California) 5.
Culture and globalization–Mexico–Tijuana (Baja California) 6. Tijuana (Baja California, Mexico)–
Ethnic relations. 7. Tijuana (Baja California, Mexico)–Social conditions. 8. Tijuana (Baja California,
Mexico)–Economic conditions. I. Title.
  F1221.M7M38 2006
  305.897′630722–dc22

                                                                            2005004407

A British Cataloging-in-Publication record for this book is available from the British Library

Manufactured in the United States of America

CONTENTS

ACKNOWLEDGMENTS

This book is the result of many years working closely with the members of my dissertation committee, Deborah Poole, Judith Friedlander, and the late William Roseberry. Deborah Poole and William Roseberry encouraged me to develop a latent interest in race, racism, and political economy and enthusiastically supported me in graduate school and beyond. I am grateful to Deborah and Gerardo Rénique for their intellectual inspiration and warm friendship. Judith Friedlander rescued me in difficult times, and readers will notice in this work the influence of her classic *Being Indian in Hueyapan: A Study of Forced Identity in Contemporary Mexico* (New York: St. Martins Press, 1975).

During fieldwork, I appreciated the support of Jorge Bustamante, who granted institutional affiliation at Colegio de la Frontera Norte. Christian Zlolniski, Alberto Hernández, and Marcela Martínez de Castro provided essential logistic support and intellectual stimulation while I was in Tijuana. Gonzalo Montiel Aguirre, Reina Ramírez, Juana Hernández, and Tomás Paz shared their friendship and knowledge. I am grateful to the Mixtec community in Baja California for their support and permission to carry out this study, which I hope is useful for them in some way. The government officials from the National Indigenist Institute, the Department of Public Education, the Department of Popular Cultures, the National Program in Solidarity with Day Laborers, and Tijuana City Hall as well as the Salesian Fathers of Tijuana, the Iglesia de Dios Israelita, the Iglesia Cristiana Armadura de Dios, and several libraries in the city of Tijuana opened their doors to me and were collaborative and friendly.

The Wenner-Gren Foundation for Anthropological Research sponsored this project with two grants (#6044 and #11301), one for fieldwork and another for postdoctoral writing (Richard Carley Hunt Post-Doctoral

Fellowship). I appreciate the foundation's continuing support, without which this project would not have been possible. The MacArthur Foundation granted a fellowship for writing at the International Center for Migration, Ethnicity, and Citizenship in New York City. I am also grateful for the long-term institutional and financial help of the New School for Social Research (now New School University).

At the New School, I profited from interaction with many professors and students in a truly stimulating intellectual environment, particularly Kate Crehan (who saved me from dangerous methodological mistakes), Steve Caton, Anthony Pereira, Xavier Andrade, Helga Baitenman, Kim Clark, Robin Lebaron, Tibisay Lucena, Ricardo Macip, Lauren Martin, Emiko Saldívar, Casey Walsh, and many others. At Northeastern University, I appreciated the advise and encouragement of Amílcar Barreto, Wini Breines, Luis Falcón, Deborah Kaufman, Maureen Kelleher, Tom Koenig, Laurie Occhipinti, Gordana Rabrenovic, Alan West-Durán, and Katrina Zippel. I am also indebted to Northeastern and to Dean James Stellar for granting a year of leave that allowed me to finish the manuscript.

Francisco Rhon and the staff of Centro Andino de Acción Popular provided institutional support, coffee, and a warm community in some phases of the writing stage. I would like to thank FLACSO-Ecuador, particularly Fernando Carrión, Felipe Burbano de Lara, and Adrián Bonilla for granting the valuable time without too many responsibilities that made possible the completion of this project. That says a lot about an institution that works with limited resources. Alex Terán helped efficiently with the maps. Steve Rubenstein, Steve Striffler, and Andrés Guerrero read the entire manuscript and offered valuable advice on how to improve it. I am also thankful to Kay Mansfield and Willa Speiser for their editorial help. Finally, I would like to thank Kristi Long and David Myers, editor and former editor at Rutgers University Press, for believing in the project.

A shorter version of chapter 2 was published as "The Making of Vulnerabilities: Indigenous Day Laborers in Mexico's Neoliberal Agriculture," *Identities* 11, no. 2 (2004): 217–241. A version of chapter 3 was published as "We Are Against the Government, Although We Are the Government. State Institutions and Indigenous Migrants in Baja California, Mexico in the 1990s," *Journal of Latin American Anthropology* 9, no. 2 (2004): 352–381.

Chapter 4 was published as "The Culture of Exclusion: Representations of Indigenous Women Street Vendors in Tijuana, Mexico," *Bulletin of Latin American Research* 22, no. 3 (2003): 249–268. Some of the empirical material in chapter 5 was used in two articles in Spanish: "Empresas Mixtecas: desarrollo y poder en una cooperativa indígena en la frontera México-Estados Unidos," in *La controversia del desarrollo: críticas desde la antropología*, edited by Juan Carlos Gimeno and Pilar Monreal (Madrid: Catarata, 1999); and "Racismo, amor y desarrollo comunitario," *Iconos: the Journal of FLACSO-Ecuador* 4 (1998): 98–110. The artwork used in the cover of this book is by Ecuadorian artist Marcelo Aguirre and is entitled "Dulce Hipocresía" (Sweet Hypocrisy). I thank Marcelo for his kindness in letting Rutgers University Press reproduce his work.

The ideas developed here reflect the influence of my parents, José Miguel Martínez and Inmaculada Novo, who taught me to dare to think differently from the majority. This book would not have been possible without the emotional, intellectual, and, at times, financial support of my husband, Carlos de la Torre, who has contributed to this project in many ways, from fieldwork to book. My children, Gabriel and Alejandro, made the process of writing much longer and difficult but also much more enjoyable and productive. I hope that, in a few years, these pages will have some meaning for them.

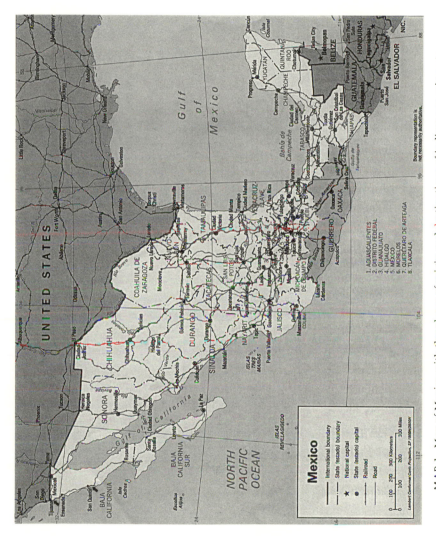

MAP 1. Map of Mexico with the places of origin and destinations of indigenous migrants.

Courtesy of the University of Texas Libraries, The University of Texas at Austin

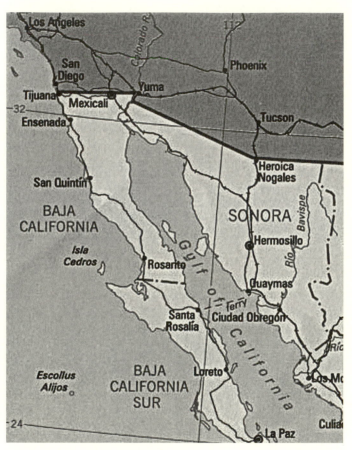

MAP 2. The State of Baja California and Surrounding Area.

Courtesy of the University of Texas Libraries, The University of Texas at Austin

Who Defines Indigenous?

Introduction

The idea for this book began to take shape in the summer of 1994 in a Chinese restaurant in the city of Tijuana, located on the northwest Mexico–United States border and in the Mexican state of Baja California. I was having lunch with a sociologist and government official who, at the time, directed one of the institutions in charge of indigenous peoples in the northwest of Mexico. I was asking him a variety of questions about indigenous peoples in Baja California when he volunteered the following information: He had organized an encounter of indigenous groups from the United States and Mexican sides of the border in his hometown, a small border town east of Tijuana. He had spoken with both indigenous leaders and the general indigenous population, rented buses to transport them to his hometown, and, as a treat, had taken some of them to the seashore for the first time in their lives. He assured me that the mountain that crowned his hometown historically had been a ceremonial site visited by indigenous groups from the region. He also confessed that the binational indigenous meeting was intended to promote the small border town and transform it into a center of attention. A few days later, I had lunch with several members of the Chamber of Commerce of the same border town. They told me that they were sponsoring a number of projects to transform the town into a cultural center to promote tourism and enhance its economy. One of these projects was the recovery of indigenous archaeological remains to strengthen the reputation of the city as an Indian ceremonial center. The town's businessmen were happy with the binational indigenous encounter organized by my government official friend because it drew attention to the border town.

A few months later, in New York, I received a copy of the journal *Abya Yala News: Journal of the South and Meso American Indian Rights Center.* That particular issue was dedicated to the relationship between state frontiers and Indian nations. I was surprised to find an article entitled "Once Divided: Indigenous Peoples in the United States and Mexico Unite Across the Border," describing the very encounter that my friend claimed to have organized (de la Peña and Bermejillo 1995, 1). The article enthusiastically emphasizes that this was a real grassroots encounter in which not only the usual leaders but also common indigenous people were present. There is no mention of state institutions involved in the encounter, despite the fact that the article is a translation of one published in Spanish in the journal of a (now defunct) Mexican state institution, the National Indigenist Institute.[1] According to de la Peña and Bermejillo, authors of the article, indigenous groups separated by the United States–Mexico border challenged both states and their boundaries. The article also states that border indigenous groups questioned capitalist projects that targeted their tribal lands. The contrast between the informal accounts of my friend and the Chamber of Commerce and how the meeting is represented in the Indian rights journal gave me the first clue that something was not what it seemed regarding the construction of indigenous identity in the northwest of Mexico.

The interpretation of the Indian rights journal resonates with a large body of scholarship that approaches identity as something that must originate from the bottom up. The reasons for the prevalence of this interpretation are complex and will be discussed at length throughout the book. Among them are the anthropological preference for a focus on the leaders of vulnerable groups whose words are taken at face value without investigating their links to more powerful institutions and actors as well as to their own constituencies. This book looks at identity from the other side: I focus on what Hill and Wilson (2003, 2) call "identity politics: the top-down processes whereby various political, economic, and other social entities attempt to mold collective identities." How do more powerful actors, particularly the state and capital—embodied in specific institutions, individuals, and groups—as well as other agents like nongovernmental organizations and intellectuals try to mold, in an imperfect and messy way, collective identities? And then, how do marginal groups respond, challenging, accommodating, or manipulating these images of themselves for their own purposes? In the earlier anecdote, state officials and capitalists did not behave as we might expect both intuitively and from previous scholarship: Instead of repressing indigenous identity or interpreting it as a challenge to their interests, government officials and the members of the Chamber of Commerce sought to support a particular understanding of Indianness that they perceived as akin to their goals. In this case, tourism was behind their interest in the promotion of identity. I will show that other economic interests, such as commercial agriculture for export, benefit from the reinforcement of Indian identification. Ironically, "indigenous" is a label that many migrants in Baja California try to flee from because, in their particular context, it functions as a stigma that hinders socioeconomic mobility. A similar phenomenon has been documented elsewhere: in a fascinating study of the culture and political economy of native Alaskans, Kirk Dombrowski (2001) argues that although native status does benefit some individuals, many others have opted to be against a culture that they consider very much their own. They have used their membership to Pentecostal churches to express these "anticultural" feelings because the Pentecostals in Alaska have emphasized the universality of humankind and have specifically rejected certain stereotypical construction of what it means to be native. Dombrowski (2001, 183) suggests, "Those from whom cultural reproduction exacts a particularly high price—those whose participation is the most tenuous, and so who are forced to absorb the greatest emotional, economic, or political risk in participating in culture—are apt to be the ones most frequently confronted by their own anticultural feelings."

This book is also an exploration of the articulations between global processes, the state, capital, and identity formation among vulnerable groups. A widespread assumption in the 1980s and 1990s was that the weakening of the state in the context of globalization—as at an international border or in a situation of national and international migration—allowed for the emergence of subnational identities that further debilitated the nation-state (Appadurai 1990; Kearney 1996a). Begoña Aretxaga (2003) has more recently argued that processes of globalization, far from weakening the state as scholars assumed during the 1980s and mid-1990s, have fueled the desire for statehood and strengthened the re-pressive capability of the state. I show throughout the book that the state has not only turned out to be more efficient in its ability to repress or to become an object of desire but has retained the ability to shape subjects to adapt to novel global situations. I will argue that what has been termed a failure of the Mexican state to control the production of identities at its borders (Kearney 1991) is sometimes, although not univocally or without contradictions, the very effect of the work of state officials and institutions, on behalf of local and global capital.

I returned to Baja California two years after the event described earlier and decided to study what it meant to be an Indian at the Mexico–United States border. Both before and after the Spanish conquest, Baja California has been sparsely populated due, among other factors, to its arid climate. Native indigenous peoples were further decimated by epidemics when they were concentrated in missions during the colonial period, and they are almost extinct today, although the few left are in the process of rein-venting themselves (see Garduño 2003). In 1970, before indigenous migra-tion from the south of Mexico to Baja California started, there were only 2,096 speakers of indigenous languages (INEGI 1990). According to the 2000 census, there are only 82 Cochimí and 178 Cucapá left, divided be-tween the states of Baja California and Sonora. The Kumiai and Paipai of Baja California have also nearly disappeared (Serrano, Embriz, and Fernández 2002).

I decided to focus on indigenous migrants, particularly the Mixtecs, a group from southwest Mexico that has migrated in large numbers to the northwest of Mexico and to the United States for more than five decades. A focus on migrants would allow me to explore how indigenous identity is shaped in the context of migration and cultural change in a dynamic, export-oriented economic area where neoliberal policies were first tried worldwide in industry and agriculture (Fernández-Kelly 1983; Thrupp 1995) and at an international border. The study of identity formation among in-digenous migrants is significant because indigenous Latin Americans are migrating in growing numbers to cities, areas of commercial agriculture, and internationally (Wade 1997). The study of Mixtec migration was popu-larized by Michael Kearney and Carole Nagengast in the early to mid–1990s (Kearney 1988, 1991, 1995, 1996a, 1996b; Nagengast and Kearney 1990).

Nagengast and Kearney portray the Mixtecs as a truly transnational group that allows for the study of indigenous identities in global contexts. A number of authors have followed them in the study of Mixtec migrants (Besserer 1997; Lestage 1998; Rhett-Mariscal 1998; Velasco1995, 2002). Challenging earlier work inspired by modernization theory that expected indigenous migrants to assimilate into the mainstream, Kearney, Nagengast, and other scholars after them argue that indigenous migrants reinforced their identity in the process of migration. They interpret this phenomenon as a way that indigenous migrants resist discrimination by the state and capitalist employers in the north of Mexico. Kearney (1991) also suggests that Mixtecs' transnational migratory experience gives them greater leeway vis-à-vis the state and allows them to develop successful subnational identities that would not have been possible had they been isolated in Mexico. In other words, the state is weakened in the context of globalization and has lost some of its ability to shape national subjects.

Kearney's work resonates with work on identity and globalization popular in the 1990s. For example, Arjun Appadurai (1990, 1996) notes that one of the consequences of globalization was the "deterritorializaton" and loss of roots of individuals. This situation produced deep feelings of alienation that were compensated by what Appadurai calls "local fetishism," which might include the reinforcement of identities based on ethnicity, regionalism, or religion. In other words, in a context of deracination and alienation, common people take refuge in traditional identities that provide them with feelings of security and belonging. The reinforcement of "local fetishism," Appadurai argues, is facilitated by improvements in communication and transportation technologies that allow the rapid transfer of images and ideas, and by the crisis of nation-states that became unable to control what takes place within their borders, including the production of subnational identities. Thus, Appadurai, like Kearney, understands the reinforcement of ethnic identity as a challenge for a weakened nation-state in the context of globalization.

Inspired by the work of Kearney and other scholars of identity formation in global contexts, I expected to find a vibrant indigenous movement struggling for indigenous rights and against the exploitation of border employers. I also expected to see the Mexican government repress this movement on behalf of capitalists. Paradoxically, I found government officials

organizing and funding indigenous groups and insisting that migrants remain so identified. This happened in a context in which those labeled as
Indians constitute cheap labor in commercial agriculture, construction,
and gardening or join the informal economy. Meanwhile, many grassroots
Mixtecs that I met during fieldwork were reluctant to pursue this agenda,
because they preferred to melt in, avoid the stigma attached to the label
"Indian," and seek social mobility. Those among indigenous migrants
wishing to push an ethnic agenda were leaders and intellectuals, many of
whom were trained by the state, worked for the state, and promoted state
agendas. Others were union leaders whose organizations eventually developed close ties with state institutions (Millán and Rubio 1992). This book
pinpoints a key problem in the investigation of Mixtec migrant identity:
the agendas of indigenous community leaders are often taken for
grassroots points of view in the literature. I suggest that the complex intermediate position of indigenous migrant leaders is a critical part of the
story. In addition, union movements that are not necessarily ethnic, such
as Central Independiente de Obreros Agrícolas y Campesinos (CIOAC) [In-
dependent Union of Agrarian Workers and Peasants], a nationwide organization,[2] are counted as indigenous movements by some scholars (Kearney
1988; Nagengast and Kearney 1990; Velasco 2002). Laura Velasco (2002)
uses the number of ethnic organizations and interviews with the leaders of
these organizations as proof of the strength and grassroots character of indigenous migrant identity without taking into account the number of followers of these organizations and whether these organizations had
developed close links to the state by the 1990s. Finally, I observed that
much of what was identified and promoted as "indigenous culture" by
government-appointed and other advocates was either a stereotypical construction of "Indianness" that had little to do with the actual experiences of
Mixtec migrants or a manifestation of poverty that was naturalized as
culture.

The data from the 2000 Mexican census are intriguing in relation to
indigenous identity in Baja California. According to the census, the number of indigenous people living in Baja California has increased from approximately 2,000 in the 1970s to 80,984. This represents 3.3 percent of the
total population of the state: 56.7 percent of these people are migrants
born outside the state. Forty-one percent of those labeled indigenous were

born in Baja California, but most are second- or third-generation migrants. Less than half of the total number of those labeled indigenous speak a native language (37,685), and 96.8 percent of speakers of native languages are bilingual in Spanish. The majority of those who speak a native language speak Mixtec (14,184). The second language spoken in the state, Zapotec, has 2,990 speakers.

According to classic post-Revolutionary definitions of Indian status in Mexico, such as that offered by Alfonso Caso (1980),[3] an Indian who leaves his or her community and learns Spanish becomes *mestizo* ("mixed blood")[4] because speaking a native language and living in a community defined as indigenous have been the preferred markers of official Indian status. Using this definition, the 42,299 migrants who do not speak a native language would definitely have been labeled mestizo, as might those who are bilingual in Spanish and a native language and live outside their territory of origin. Only the 1,146 people who are monolingual in a native language, and perhaps the small group of native Baja Californians who speak an indigenous language and live in their original territory, would qualify as indigenous according to classical definitions. The 2000 census, however, uses a combination of criteria that reflects an important change in official markers of ethnicity in Mexico. Census makers keep language as an important trait, and they add self-definition and belonging to an indigenous home; according to census makers, a home where the head of household, or his or her partner, or any of their parents on either side speak an indigenous language or self-identify as indigenous (see Serrano, Embriz, and Fernández 2002).[5] Why are these people now labeled indigenous after a process of migration and cultural change that includes the loss of the mother tongue? Are they labeled indigenous based on self-definition? If so, why do they choose to define themselves as indigenous? If the number of indigenous people originates in self-definition, why do census makers need the "indigenous home" indicator? Is it a substitute for the earlier "indigenous community" in a context of massive migration of indigenous peasants to cities and areas of commercial agriculture? And why have definitions of Indian status changed in Mexico and Baja California to become more inclusive?

This book attempts to show what it means to be an "indigenous migrant" in particular historical and political-economic conjunctures. In this,

I am inspired by Omi and Winant's (1986) concept of racial formation, "the sociohistorical process by which racial categories are created, inhabited, transformed, and destroyed." Other authors (for example, Harrison 1999; Poole 1997; Rénique 2003; Stephen 1991, 1996; Wade 1998) have also insisted that race and ethnicity should be understood in concrete historical and political economic contexts. I choose two contexts in which to study the meaning of "indigenous migrant." The first is the valley of San Quintín, where indigenous migrants are the preferred labor force in export-oriented agriculture; the second is the city of Tijuana, the site of a conflict between indigenous women street vendors, merchants, other members of the middle class, and municipal authorities for the control of the spaces that support a dynamic tourist economy. I look at the diversity of discourses (discourses published in books and the press and those expressed by informants in daily conversations) that arise from these contexts of conflict and analyze the relationship between representations of race and ethnicity by non-Indians and the indigenous migrant community and the struggle for the distribution of resources along racial or ethnic lines. I follow here Omi and Winant's (2002, 124–125) concept of racial project, which they define as "simultaneously an interpretation, representation, or explanation of racial dynamics, and an effort to reorganize and redistribute resources along particular racial lines."

How does this book relate to the larger literature on globalization and indigenous identity? There are two approaches to the topic. A number of authors argue that globalization has negatively affected indigenous people (for example, Brysk 2000; Nash 2001; Sieder 2002; Stephen 2002; Zamosc 1994). These authors understand globalization to be internationally imposed regressive economic policies, such as the end of subsidies for the acquisition of basic products and subsidies to national producers; the contraction of the public budget for social services; an emphasis on exports that destroys the environment inhabited by indigenous groups or that only benefits dynamic sectors of the bourgeoisie at the expense of small producers; the promotion of privatization and free trade in general; and so on. These authors tend to interpret the reinforcement of indigenous identity in recent decades as an organizational tool with which to resist these economic transformations. According to these authors, identification as Indians helps vulnerable groups emancipate themselves from the oppression of nation-states and an international context that promotes a renewed version of capitalism.

A number of scholars also acknowledge that globalization has opened windows of opportunity for indigenous peoples. Alyson Brysk (2000) describes the formation of a "global civil society" that watches for the rights of indigenous peoples and funds their initiatives. Lynn Stephen (1991, 1996), Rudi Colloredo-Mansfeld (1999), and David Kyle (2000), among others, have discussed how groups of indigenous entrepreneurs have been able to take advantage of global capitalism by exporting their crafts and culture at considerable gain. According to these authors, the prosperity thus acquired has reinforced, although not left unchanged, their ethnic identity. In some cases indigenous people resist capitalism, in others they take advantage of it. In both situations the reinforcement of indigenous identity benefits marginalized groups.

There are fewer works about how racialization (the application of racial and ethnic labels to certain groups) may have negative effects for those so identified in the context of globalization. Karen Brodkin's (1998) article "Global Capitalism: What's Race Got to Do With It?" reflects on how state and global capitalist projects have dovetailed to racialize people as nonwhite to make them vulnerable and favor their economic exploitation. She uses the example of Jewish Americans who changed from white to nonwhite and then to white again as their relations to the means of production changed. Kirk Dombrowski (2001) also discusses how the imposition of certain ways of being Indian and not others on native Alaskans by United States legislation facilitated the extraction of resources like oil, timber, and fish by corporations. In the Mexican context, Luis Vazquez León (2003; forthcoming) has suggested that there is an official interest in keeping migrant day laborers Indian, as export-oriented agriculture, fueled by the availability of cheap indigenous workers, becomes central to the Mexican economy. The present book contributes to this less-explored aspect of the formation of indigenous identity in global contexts. I do not necessarily challenge those authors who conceive indigenous identity as a tool for emancipation. I argue that the meaning of "Indianness," as well as other identities, needs to be considered in particular contexts. Whereas Indian identification may be beneficial for groups of craftsmen and women who have been able to take advantage of the taste for the exotic in a global economy, or for well-organized indigenous movements fighting regressive economic and social policies, it may still be strongly associated with stigmatization and overexploitation in other political-economic contexts.

Racism and Paternalism

When I first went to the field, my main concern was the study of the formation of indigenous migrant identities. However, I soon realized that it was important to pay attention to different but related phenomena: racism and its sweetened version, paternalism. This book is to a large degree a study of racism as it took shape in the north of Mexico and affected the indigenous migrant population in the late 1990s. The purpose of my work is not just to prove that there is racism in the north of Mexico, as racism is often associated in the north with the United States or with the more hierarchical south,[6] but to explore the particular ways in which racism is expressed and the concrete mechanisms through which the indigenous population is stereotyped and excluded from resources and opportunities. I look at two sites of discrimination—the valley of San Quintín and the city of Tijuana—and discuss the differences and similarities in patterns of discrimination in these two contexts. Some of these differences are gendered; day laborers working in San Quintín are most of the time imagined by scholars and the press to be men (although more than half of them are women!), whereas in the urban context women are more visible than men in the discourses of the press, merchants, and the middle class. I agree with Omi and Winant (2002) that racism, like race, changes historically and varies in different locations. Thus, it is important to study racism in its specific historical and political-economic circumstances. However, I also trace some continuities between present-day discrimination in the north of Mexico and colonial and postcolonial understandings of the Indian. Finally, I argue that in the north of Mexico, discourses of race (essentialist representations based on supposed physical differences) and discourses of ethnicity (essentialist representations based on supposed cultural differences) are intertwined and complement each other to justify the exclusion of indigenous migrants.

Particularly important for an understanding of the specificities of forms of discrimination in Mexico is a focus on paternalism—or maternalism when the dominant party is a woman, as it frequently happens given the construction of elite women as those who should take care of the vulnerable. Discourses that have discriminatory effects are constructed as manifestations of love for indigenous people who are represented as childish and naïve, lovable but definitely not equal. The phenomenon of paternalism has been explored by scholars of the United States South and by philosophers (Chan 2000; Jackman 1994; Van der Veer 1986; Weiner 1986; Wingerd 1996) but it is understudied in the anthropological literature as well as in the literature on race and ethnicity in Latin America and elsewhere. For example, in a recent book on critical theories of race edited by Essed and Goldberg (2002), the word "paternalism" does not even appear in the index. Moreover, according to Peter Wade's (1997) exhaustive review of the literature on race and ethnicity in Latin America, there are only a few scattered references to paternalism. Nor has the anthropological literature focused enough on this phenomenon. Three anthropological studies of elites have only passing references to this topic (Adler Lomnitz and Pérez Lizaur 1987; Cohen 1981; Shore and Nugent 2002). An exception in the anthropological literature is Sherry Ortner's (1999a) *Life and Death in Mount Everest,* in which she describes the paternalism of Western explorers toward the Sherpas of the Himalayas.

Pierre Van der Berghe defines paternalism in a classic comparative study on race and racism in Mexico, Brazil, the United States, and South Africa. In a modernization theory style, Van der Berghe (1967, 27) divides systems of race relations into paternalistic and competitive systems. According to him, in a paternalistic system,

> The dominant group . . . rationalizes its rule in an ideology of benevolent despotism and regards members of the subordinate group as childish, immature, irresponsible . . . in short, as inferior but lovable as long as they stay "in their place." In the subordinate group there is in general an ostensible accommodation to inferior status and sometimes even an interiorization of inferiority feelings. . . . Roles and statuses are sharply defined along racial lines, with a rigidly ascriptive division of labor and a great asymmetry and complementarity in social relationships. Social distance between racial castes is maximized and symbolized by an elaborate and

punctilious etiquette involving nonreciprocal terms of address, sumptuary regulations, and repeated manifestations of subservience and dominance. This great degree of social distance allows close symbiosis and even intimacy, without any threat to status inequalities. Consequently, physical segregation is not prominently used as a mechanism of social control. Prejudice often takes the form of "pseudo-tolerance" as exemplified by professions of love for the subordinate group as long as inequality is unchallenged.

Van der Berghe believes that paternalistic race relations characterize traditional agrarian societies, and that they will be eventually superseded by competitive race relations (more democratic, but more violent, such as those that, according to Van der Berghe, characterized the United States during the 1960s) and ultimately by racial democracy. My book argues that systems of social relations conceived as traditional have the ability to adapt surprisingly well to new contexts. More recently, Mary Jackman (1994) has written an interesting account of paternalism in gender, class, and race relations centered in the United States. Like Van der Berghe, Jackman defines paternalism as the phenomenon of discrimination without the expression of hostility as long as the subordinate party stays in his or her place. However, unlike Van der Berghe, she shows that paternalism is a pervasive and resilient contemporary phenomenon, at least in the United States. My book focuses to a large degree on the study of paternalistic discourses and practices and their discriminatory effects.

Methodology

This book is an exercise in "studying up" (Nader 1969), the critical ethnography of elites or powerful people and institutions. It does not focus only on subordinate groups as do many anthropological works. My purpose is not to write a piece on Mixtec migrants who have already been discussed elsewhere (Garduño, García, and Morán 1989; Kearney 1996a; Lestage 1998; Millán and Rubio 1992; Rhett-Mariscal 1998; Velasco 1995, 2002) but to focus on the attitudes and practices of those who interact with them. My subjects are government officials, elite and middle-class women who work for a nongovernmental organization, merchants, anthropologists and sociologists, journalists, and indigenous leaders. The work that I did with

grassroots indigenous people was intended to contrast with and complement the representations and misrepresentations of them by non-Indians,
but it was not intended to be the basis of the study. The study of non-
Indians who interact with indigenous people is relevant to the exploration
of two themes that constitute the core of this book: the impact of external
influences in the construction of indigenous migrant identity, and the
anatomy of racism and paternalism as they appear in the Baja Californian
context and affect indigenous migrants. Laura Nader (1969) wrote about
the "perspectives gained from studying up." She claims that anthropologists should produce work that is concerned with the exercise of power and
that has democratic relevance. To learn about power, Nader argues, we
should study those who exercise it. She argues that to study up may provide
theoretical perspectives on social relations, the nature of oppression, and
the deployment of power that are simply lost when we focus exclusively on
subordinate groups. A book on elite cultures by Shore and Nugent (2002)
recovers Nader's argument. However, more than three decades have
elapsed since Nader made her statement, and there is still little to show
from this perspective in the anthropological record. Nader's and Shore and
Nugent's argument resonates with a literature that has emphasized the
need to study anthropological subjects not as if they were isolated (which
they are not), but within larger contexts, historical processes, and wider
sets of social relations (Friedlander 1975; Muratorio 1991; Poole 1997;
Roseberry 1989; Wolf 1982).

Both Nader and Shore and Nugent point out that access is not easy
when anthropologists study up because those with a relative amount of
power are able to control both access to them and how they are represented. I solved this problem by becoming an "external agent" myself. I
started to participate in a nongovernmental organization that worked with
indigenous migrants. I thought that the best way to understand external
agents and their worldviews was to work with them. However, I was not
paid by the organization, because I was funded by a scholarship from a
North American foundation. In this way, I avoided ethical problems, and I
could be more independent while doing research and writing.

My location at the organization opened the doors of governmental institutions and connected me to other informants. In addition, it was easier
for the indigenous migrant community to place me, because I had a

defined function in the neighborhood: I taught reading and writing and later English to indigenous and mestizo neighbors as a member of this nongovernmental organization. I played a concrete role in the community and therefore was not that alien or unclassifiable to them. Thus, I could contribute something to the community while doing fieldwork. I verbally informed the nongovernmental organization and the research center that sponsored it that I was studying their program, and I gave them a written copy of my dissertation proposal that clearly stated that I intended to study their development work. I also explained my project to the rest of my informants, such as government officials, merchants, indigenous migrants, and so on. I let everybody know that I was studying their work with or their approach to indigenous migrants, and not the indigenous community in and of itself. It is interesting that most of them did not take what I said seriously. Their strong assumptions about the nature of anthropological work made them believe that I should be researching the indigenous community.

In Mexico, the work of anthropologists is well known because many have collaborated with revolutionary governments since the early twentieth century. Some have reached prominent positions in government, such as secretary of agriculture or education. The role of anthropologists in the revolutionary project has been to articulate indigenous people to a fractured nation (Hewitt de Alcántara 1984). Thus, the association of anthropology with the study of the Indian is strong. Some shrewd government officials, as well as other people with whom I came in contact, were well aware of what I was doing but tried to convince me to change my focus to the indigenous community and its process of "acculturation."

The fact that I come from Spain helped me in contacting informants. The colonial past of Mexico makes Spain and everything related to it a symbol of status. The more elitist my informants were, the more they wanted to relate to a Spaniard. Paradoxically, the cultural legacy of colonialism helped me to gain access to my information, and being a Spaniard did not pose any problems that I am aware of in communicating with indigenous migrants. The only thing that I noticed in this respect is that teachers would change topics at the indigenous bilingual school when they were teaching about Spanish colonialism and I entered the room.

Because I became an external agent, I became so identified. Community people who disliked the approach of the nongovernmental organization with which I collaborated distrusted me. My point of entrance into the community also limited the kinds of information that I was able to get. I believe this problem was unavoidable. To get one kind of information, I had to renounce another. However, this problem did not worry me too much, because my purpose was to focus to a large degree on external agents. In addition, by the end of my stay in Tijuana, I became more independent from the nongovernmental organization and did more research alone.

I have been urged by various scholars who have read my work to examine my own role more in different chapters of the book. I have done so when I have felt that it was important from a methodological and theoretical point of view to understand how my interaction with informants may have affected the information that I was able to get. However, my priority has been to understand social interactions at the Mexican border independent of my own peripheral role in them. Therefore, I deliberately kept a low profile and let informants talk without too many interferences. On the other hand, I do appreciate an anthropology that challenges the myth of the objective outside observer, and I do position myself: I am a Spaniard who spent her early years under the Franco dictatorship and the transition to democracy and whose family, school, and neighborhood environments, of working- and middle-class origins, were made up of critical antidictatorship activists. This background has allowed me to be comfortable when moving against the current. In the United States, particularly when I started to work, I was constructed as a minority person. This way I learned some of what it means to be undervalued and discriminated against. The fact that I am a woman played a role as well. However, my structural position changes radically in Latin America, where I become "white" as a representative of the colonial metropolis. Despite the fact that I acknowledge the importance of positioning myself, I am also worried about an anthropology in which the author invades the text, which then becomes an exercise in self-reflection. Again, I am clear that my main objective is to learn about what is going on in the field and not so much about what I feel about it, although, obviously, my own feelings and judgments, influenced by a particular background and position, can not and should not be ignored.

Besides participant observation as an "external agent," I have used a variety of sources of information to complete this book. I visited Baja California every year from 1993 to 1996, and I spent the academic year 1996–1997 in the field. I complemented participant observation with recorded in-depth interviews, life histories, and oral histories with a variety of informants—external agents, indigenous leaders, and grassroots community members. I combined ethnography with archival research. I reviewed five local newspapers from the early 1980s to the late 1990s to gather information about indigenous migrants and those who interacted with them and about representations of indigenous migrants in the local press. I also gathered information from a couple of national newspapers. The history that emerged from newspaper accounts helped me interpret ethnographic data. I was able to ask my informants better questions and to distance myself from some of their answers. However, it was a two-way process because informants let me know about important historical conjunctures and conflicts to heed and more fruitful ways to interpret press accounts.

Organization of the Book

This book is organized as follows: chapter 1 provides a context in which to understand the history and role of indigenous migrants in Baja California. Chapter 2 discusses a riot of indigenous day laborers in the San Quintín Valley. Combining press accounts of the riot with ethnography, I look at the intersections between global processes, local social relations, and cultural representations of race and ethnicity. I examine how representations of race, ethnicity, gender, and region are deployed to account for a segmented labor system, and I explore how the modern agro-export sector takes advantage of and reshapes social relations of colonial origin that are most often associated with tradition. In chapter 3, I discuss three state institutions that work with indigenous migrants in Baja California: the National Indianist Institute, the General Directorate of Indigenous Education of the Department of Public Education, and the Department of Popular Cultures. I look at the strategies used by these institutions to reinforce indigenous identity, and I explore what government officials mean by indigenous culture and social organization. The chapter ends with a reflection on how the populist state is organized. Chapter 4 focuses on a conflict among indigenous women street vendors, merchants, and other members of the middle class and municipal authorities. The debate that arises from this conflict serves as the basis for a reflection on the uses of culture and gender norms as constructed by the mainstream to exclude indigenous women from economic opportunities in the border economy. Chapter 5 discusses the impact on the reinforcement of class and race hierarchies at the Mexican border of a nongovernmental organization that offers the labor force of indigenous women to transnational capital for assembly tasks. Because this nongovernmental organization is directed by an elite Mexican woman and staffed by middle-class women, I use these data to reflect on the complex and gendered interactions between elites, middle classes, and the indigenous migrant community. The book's conclusion discusses the relationship between cultural differences and democracy. It also discusses the ways in which representations of indigenous migrants, both hostile (racist) and apparently benign (paternalistic), by institutions, intellectuals, elites, middle classes, and the press are linked to the exclusion of this community from resources and opportunities.

The names of informants as well as some biographical details and references have been omitted or changed to protect their privacy, but I have preserved the names of some informants when citing their publications or the documents written by them, or in those cases in which I felt that mentioning their names would not cause them any inconvenience. The purpose of this book is not to accuse or judge particular individuals and institutions but to try to understand social relations in a particular place at a particular time. All translations of interviews and texts are mine.

1

▶▶▶▶▶▶▶▶▶▶▶▶▶ ◀◀◀◀◀◀◀◀◀◀◀◀◀

Mixtec Communities
at the Mexican Border

Before Spanish colonization, the Baja California peninsula was sparsely populated by hunting, fishing, and gathering native groups referred to as Cochimís or Yumans (León Portilla 1970, 1972). The peninsula was discovered by the Europeans in an expedition sent by Hernán Cortés in 1532. During the sixteenth and seventeenth centuries, Spanish adventurers carried out several failed expeditions to Baja California. Although Europeans coveted its abundant fish and pearls, the peninsula was too arid to sustain either a large native or European population. For these reasons, Baja California was not settled definitively until the eighteenth century. Jesuit missionaries, who had already colonized the neighboring coasts of Sonora and Sinaloa, undertook this challenging task. Across the peninsula, the Jesuits created a network of missions at which the native population congregated. Subsequent epidemics decimated mission Indians, and at the end of the eighteenth century the Jesuits were expelled from New Spain. As a result, the Baja Californian peninsula became depopulated and was abandoned by the colonial state.

After Mexico achieved independence from Spain in 1822, the northern region remained unpopulated and isolated from the rest of the country because of poor overland communication with the capital city. The newly formed Mexican government was affected by too many uprisings and civil wars for it to worry about the arid, depopulated, and remote northern provinces, which were constantly threatened by native resistance and the expansion of the United States. The war with the United States resulted in the annexation of California, Arizona, New Mexico, and Texas by the United States in 1848. After the war, Baja California remained even more isolated from Mexico and started to have greater contact with the United States than with the central government of Mexico, a pattern that has lasted until recent decades. The late nineteenth century was a period of dependent capitalist development in Baja California. The government of Porfirio Díaz granted concessions to foreign companies for mining and agricultural ventures. The Colorado River Land Company developed commercial agriculture close to the border. The Santa Rosalía copper mines, located in the middle of the peninsula, were exploited by French interests.

The north of Mexico played a key role in the Mexican Revolution. A warring peasantry accustomed to fight raiding natives, filibusters, and foreign occupation, along with leaders such as Francisco Villa, Alvaro Obregón, Plutarco Elías Calles, and Venustiano Carranza, all of them northerners, were instrumental in the success and institutionalization of the Revolution (Alonso 1995; Nugent 1993). After the Revolution, the north acquired renewed importance because of its role in the revolutionary struggle and because the integration of the northern frontier was important to the processes of state formation and national consolidation. Beginning in the 1930s, the state sponsored several large irrigation projects to develop commercial agriculture in the northwest. In Baja California, President Lázaro Cárdenas (1934–1940) nationalized the lands of the Colorado River Land Company and other large properties and distributed land to peasants. Because the area was sparsely populated, Cárdenas promoted massive migration from the south. Migrant and local peasants were granted *ejidos* (inalienable land grants managed in common by peasant communities that were in this way articulated to the state). Thanks to these development efforts, the population of Baja California grew considerably from the 1930s on, and the region became increasingly integrated into the rest of Mexico. In 1947, the Sonora–Baja California Railroad connected the peninsula to the rest of Mexico by land. Some years later a road connecting Baja California to the Mexican capital was finished. The region's close relationship to the United States continued, however.

The state sponsored additional irrigation projects from the 1950s to the 1970s. These were qualitatively different from those launched in the Cárdenas period. The first were oriented toward subsistence and national urban consumption; the second looked to international markets, especially the United States. After World War II, renewed demand for vegetables and fruits in the United States fostered the development in Mexico of commercial agriculture for export (Collier 1994). The Sinaloa project, which began in the 1950s, faced the same scarcity of labor that the earlier one in the Colorado River valley had. The migrant peasants were not granted ejido land, however; on the contrary, recruiters imported indigenous day laborers from the southwestern state of Oaxaca to work under extremely exploitative conditions in the Sinaloan fields. This strategy contributed to the formation of a semiproletarianized indigenous labor force that worked part of the year in their small plots in Oaxaca and the rest as wage laborers in the north of Mexico. The San Quintín irrigation project started in the 1970s in the Baja Californian peninsula and was organized along the same lines as the Sinaloan one. In fact, some firms from Sinaloa are among the most important producers in San Quintín. The development of commercial agriculture for export brought the first communities of indigenous migrants, most of them Mixtecs, to Baja California.

How northern Mexican identity has been historically constructed produces a contrast between social relations in contemporary export-oriented agriculture and ideas about what northern society was, is, or should be. Because the indigenous population was scarce or did not easily submit to colonizers in the north of Mexico, it was not used historically as the main source of labor. This fact and the frontier character of the northern region, where peasants had to fight warring natives and foreign invaders, precluded the formation of social relations of serfdom, such as those that characterize the center and south of Mexico (Alonso 1995; León-Portilla 1972). The northern peasantry had enjoyed special freedoms and rights to property since the colonial period as a compensation for the harsh environment and the insecurity of the region (Alonso 1995; Nugent 1993). These freedoms and privileges resembled those granted in medieval Spain to peasants who agreed to live in frontier areas during the Catholic conquest of the Iberian Peninsula from the Arabs. Because of this historical legacy, northerners perceive the social conditions of exploitation that characterize commercial agriculture in Sinaloa and San Quintín as traditional imports from the hierarchical south that do not fit well in what they perceive as a more democratic and modern north. However, taking into account the evolution of agrarian policies in post-Revolutionary Mexico, there has been a shift from small-scale intensive peasant production to an increasing proletarianization of the peasantry (Collier 1994). From this point of view, peasant democracy would be traditional and day-laborer exploitation would be modern.

Ideas about northern identity also produce contrasts between northerners and immigrants from the south from the point of view of race. Because native peoples in the north resisted colonization to a large degree, settler peasants defined their identity in opposition to what they represented as savage, barbarous Indians. Missionaries, for their part, encouraged the concentration of indigenous groups in an effort to avoid genocide and extinction by settlers. This, combined with the fact that the indigenous population was much smaller in the north than in the south, precluded a widespread process of *mestizaje* (miscegenation), such as the one that took place in the center and south of Mexico (Alonso 1995). These factors all contribute to the conceptualization of the north of Mexico as a "white" region. The proximity of the United States perhaps is another factor that induces the perception of the region as "whiter" and more "modern" than the south. The representation obscures the fact that settlers mixed with local natives and that indigenous and mixed-blood peasants came from the south to settle the northern frontier. The construction of the north as "white" and the definition of its identity in opposition to "savage" Indians serve as the basis for northern Mexican racism against migrants from the south, particularly if they are indigenous. Paradoxically, the construction of the north as "white" is also used to claim that there is no racism in the area.

In 1965, the Mexican government started to promote the industrialization of the border by transnational capital. The termination of the bracero program[1] in 1964 raised unemployment rates in border cities to unbearable limits. To resolve this social crisis and develop the border region, the Mexican government facilitated the installation of foreign industries in a delimited area, relaxing the protectionist industrial policies that had characterized Mexico since the implementation of the import-substitution model in the 1930s. The Mexican government allowed "the duty-free importation of machinery, equipment, and raw materials along the Mexican border on the condition that everything produced was exported" (Fernández-Kelly 1983, 27). Transnational firms, for their part, took advantage of lower labor costs, relaxed environmental laws, and the low transportation costs that resulted from the region's proximity to the United States market. The Mexican border and Puerto Rico pioneered the transfer of industries from the developed to the developing world, a process that is much more generalized today. The first assembly industries transferred to the Mexican border were textiles and electronics (Fernández-Kelly 1983). More recently, the automobile industry has become dominant in Ciudad Juarez, and the computer industry in Tijuana (Sklair 1993). Transnational firms operating in Tijuana are not all North American, as is often believed. Capital from Japan, Korea, Canada, Mexico, and other countries is also present.

The development of the city of Tijuana is closely related to its character as a border city. During the nineteenth century, Tijuana was no more than a cattle ranch and, later, a tiny border town. In the first decades of the twentieth century the city grew with the transfer of activities that were restricted or forbidden in the United States, such as alcohol consumption and gambling (O. Martínez 1988). Tijuana gained the reputation of a city of sin and the road to hell" (Martínez 1988; Profitt 1994). At the beginning of the twentieth century, Tijuana thrived as San Diego turned into an important port with the opening of the Panama Canal. During and after World War II, San Diego became an important military base for the control of the Pacific area, and Tijuana boomed as a center of entertainment for military men. Alcohol, gambling, and prostitution flourished on the Mexican side of the border. Another source of growth for Tijuana was the number of people who arrived in the city to migrate to the United States or who were deported from the United States. Since the 1970s, the assembly industry has brought prosperity to Tijuana despite the low wages and harsh working conditions that characterize the sector (Fernández-Kelly 1983; Sklair 1993). Because many tourists cross to Tijuana from the United States to get a glimpse of Mexico, the tourist sector has become important to the economy of the city, and a relatively prosperous local class of merchants has formed. Indigenous women and children also take advantage of this economic opportunity, which creates resentment and rivalry by the middle classes, who see them as threats to their own prosperity.

The neighborhood in Tijuana where I carried out fieldwork, Colonia Valle Verde, was created by the state in 1993 to relocate poor people whose houses had been destroyed by a season of catastrophic rains. Federal, state, and local authorities collaborated in this project. For instance, President Carlos Salinas de Gortari (1989–1995) allocated funds from the Programa Nacional de Solidaridad (PRONASOL) [National Solidarity Program][2] for this purpose. The neighborhood's streets carry names inspired by the ideology of the National Solidarity Program, such as Coordination, Courage, and Cooperation.[3] Valle Verde's inhabitants are indigenous, mostly Mixtecs from Guerrero and mestizo migrants. It is interesting that state authorities resettled all indigenous people in the same sector of the neighborhood, showing again a desire to keep them from assimilating. I worked in Valle Verde because it was the neighborhood chosen by the nongovernmental organization that targeted indigenous migrants with which I collaborated. Valle Verde was the neighborhood where many indigenous women who begged or sold candies and crafts in the tourist area lived. Guerrero Mixtecs are a more recent migratory wave than Oaxacan Mixtecs, who live in Colonia Obrera, the first indigenous migrant settlement in Tijuana, which dates from the early 1970s and is a neighborhood where I also did fieldwork.

Valle Verde was created on lands of Ejido Matamoros, which had been granted to Baja Californian peasants by President Lázaro Cárdenas in 1937. The neighborhood has approximately seven thousand inhabitants (Solís Domínguez 1998) and is located in the northeastern margin of the city of Tijuana, next to the U.S. border and close to the industrial area of the city. Most of the neighborhood houses are constructed by their inhabitants from scraps of wood, tin plates, cardboard, and plastic. As the neighborhood becomes older and more settled, some of its inhabitants have been able to buy construction materials and build brick and cement houses. When I did fieldwork, Valle Verde's streets were not paved and it lacked basic services of running water and drainage. However, most of its houses already had electricity, which was often stolen from public lines (Solís Domínguez 1998).

Political competition in the state of Baja California in the 1990s had a considerable impact on the issues raised in this book. In 1989 Baja California became the first state in Mexico to be ruled by the conservative Catholic opposition party Partido de Acción Nacional (PAN) [National Action Party]. The experience of ruling in Baja California and later in other states mostly, but not exclusively, located in the northern region, helped PAN reach the presidency of Mexico in the year 2000. Many municipal governments in Baja California, including those of Tijuana and San Quintín, were also controlled by the PAN-ist opposition after 1989. Partido Revolucionario Institucional (PRI) [Revolutionary Institutional Party] ruled at the federal level in the 1990s, as it had done for more than seven decades after the consolidation of the Mexican Revolution. PAN won state and municipal elections in Baja California in 1989, the year when President Salinas de Gortari from PRI rose to power under generalized accusations of electoral fraud (Guillén 1992). Indigenous migrants have played an important symbolic role in the political competition between both parties in Baja California, because they are conceived as pillars of Mexican post-Revolutionary nationalism. After 1986, PRI, through federal government institutions that distributed funds, such as the National Indigenist Institute and the National Solidarity Program, started to co-opt indigenous organizations that were originally close to the left-wing opposition party Partido de la Revolución Democrática (PRD) [Party of the Democratic Revolution]. PRI's work with indigenous migrants intensified after the PAN-ist victory and included several visits by President Salinas de Gortari to Baja California during which he personally spoke to indigenous migrants and visited their neighborhoods. PRI used indigenous migrants politically against PAN, accusing the party of insensitivity toward popular and ethnic demands. PAN, for its part, had formerly used the harsh situation of indigenous migrants in Baja California to accuse PRI of corruption and social insensitivity before 1989, as was discussed in length in the weekly newspaper *Zeta* in the late 1980s.

Mixtecs arrive in Baja California from some of the poorest states of the Mexican southwest: Oaxaca and Guerrero. They started to migrate to the north of Mexico in the late 1960s to work in export-oriented commercial agriculture in the San Quintín Valley and in construction in the city of Tijuana, which was expanding at the time, thanks to the impulse of border industrialization, among other factors. Some Mixtecs arrived in the borderlands to migrate temporarily or definitively to the United States, where they found work as day laborers, gardeners, or service workers in California, Oregon, Florida, and New York (Kearney 1996a; Smith 1996; Stephen 2001). Some Mixtecs chose to live in Tijuana and commute daily to work in the United States after their migratory situation was regularized by the Immigration Regularization and Control Act (IRCA) in 1986. IRCA allotted visas to those who had been in the United States for a period of time while increasing control over the arrival of newcomers (Young 1994). Mixtec workers are in high demand in certain sectors, such as commercial agriculture, gardening, construction, and services, because employers consider them a docile and cheap labor force.

The Mixtec community in Tijuana is concentrated in two neighborhoods: Colonia Obrera and Valle Verde. Colonia Obrera is inhabited by older waves of Mixtec migrants from the state of Oaxaca. They are prosperous compared to newer waves of migrants, because a number have visas to cross to the United States and Oaxacan women have enough funds to invest in crafts that they sell in the tourist center of Tijuana. Newer migrants, most of them from the state of Guerrero, are settling in Colonia Valle Verde. They tend to be poorer and work as day laborers in construction, as street peddlers, or as beggars. Mixtecs use the city of Tijuana as a middle point from which they migrate to the fields of Baja California and Sinaloa or the United States (Velasco 1995). A number of Mixtec women and children take advantage of the affluence of tourists from the neighboring country to Tijuana to sell crafts, candies, or beg in the center of the city.

In the early 1980s, Mixtec migrants alone or with the help of non-Indians started several organizations to struggle for better working and living conditions in Baja California. Day laborers working in export-oriented agriculture in the San Quintín Valley created a section of CIOAC.[4] This union, sympathetic to the PRD, was quite radical in the early 1980s and faced outright repression, including, by the mid-1980s, the disappearance of some of its leaders (Nagengast and Kearney 1990). According to Garduño, García, and Morán (1989), in the late 1980s CIOAC functioned more as an urban social movement that requested the legalization of day laborers' settlements and infrastructure and services from the state than as a worker's union. This was due to fear of violence from agrarian entrepreneurs who employed armed guards to threaten workers (Rhett-Mariscal 1998).

In the second half of the 1980s, CIOAC became increasingly fragmented into several organizations that were eventually co-opted by official institutions, such as the National Indigenist Institute, which depended on the federal government. This fragmentation was caused by fights among leaders that, according to some scholars, were encouraged by the funding strategies of the federal government (Millán and Rubio 1992). CIOAC was a union of day laborers, many but not all of whom were indigenous, and it originally had a class-based approach. The smaller groups that formed later as spin-offs of CIOAC tended to emphasize ethnicity to a greater degree than the original union, in part because they were encouraged to do so by the National Indigenist Institute that funded them (interviews by author with day laborers, San Quintín, August 1997). In Tijuana, Víctor Clark, a Mexican mestizo anthropologist, and a group of Mixtec teachers brought from Oaxaca by the department of public education in 1983 formed Asociación de Mixtecos Residentes en Tijuana (ASMIRT) [Association of Mixtecs Living in Tijuana]. This group fought for street vending permits and services and infrastructure for the neighborhoods where Mixtec migrants lived. Like CIOAC, ASMIRT became fragmented into several groups in the late 1980s because of disagreements among the leadership. Some of these groups were also co-opted by official unions or the PRI by the late 1980s (Millán and Rubio 1992). When I was doing fieldwork, urban organizations collaborated with PAN, which controlled Tijuana's city hall. Indigenous organizations did not feel that they should pay exclusive allegiance to a single political party; they wanted to get benefits and support from several parties (interview by author with Mixtec leader, 1996).

2

▶▶▶▶▶▶▶▶▶▶▶▶ ◀◀◀◀◀◀◀◀◀◀◀◀

The Making of Vulnerabilities

Indigenous Day Laborers in Mexico's Neoliberal Agriculture

Introduction

This chapter focuses on representations of race and culture in the San Quintín Valley, which produces tomatoes, other vegetables, and fruits (nontraditional agro-exports)[1] for United States markets. Relatively wealthy Mexican entrepreneurs contract their production with North American firms such as Campbell's and Del Monte (contract farming)[2] or sell their products directly across the border through subsidiary firms (Garduño, García, and Morán 1989; Ortiz and Vélez 1992). Mexican entrepreneurs hire peasant families from the southern states of Oaxaca and Guerrero, some of whom speak the Mixtec language,[3] through the *enganche*[4] system to work in the fields. Meanwhile, young women from the neighboring northern state of Sinaloa are offered selection and packing jobs. Their wages typically are twice those of field workers. In Baja California, these women are considered white, in contrast to migrants from the south of Mexico, who are stigmatized as darker mestizo or Indian. White or mestizo Baja Californian men fill full-time managerial positions.

To show how ideas of race, culture, and region are deployed to account for this segmented labor organization, I look at representations of day laborers and Baja Californian export-oriented commercial agriculture in the local and national press. I contrast press accounts with fieldwork, interviews, and secondary literature. I focus particularly on a day laborers' riot or social uprising that took place in the summer of 1996.[5] The press debate that followed the events exposed the articulation between local cultural

27

images and global political-economic processes, what William Roseberry (1989), inspired by the work of the Latin American intellectuals Darcy Ribeiro and Fernando Henrique Cardoso, called "the internalization of the external." I also consider the possibility of "the externalization of the internal." As Steve Striffler (2002) has shown, local struggles and social relations can have an important effect on global capitalist processes. Striffler shows that peasant struggles for land and agrarian reform and the aloofness, incoherence, or populism of Ecuadorian state officials forced the United Fruit Company to leave direct production, restructure, and subcontract local banana producers, who then subcontracted their own temporary and precarious labor. The result was not what workers sought, but their actions did have an effect on the global restructuring of an important agrarian sector. Inspired by these concerns, I ask: How are export-oriented agriculture of nontraditional staples and the segmented labor market associated with it interpreted in the Baja Californian and Mexican contexts? How do transnational contract agriculture and regional and national social relations affect each other? In what ways do local social relations and cultural interpretations affect the organization of land and labor in transnational contract agriculture? And, on the other hand, how does export-oriented agriculture reshape and transform local understandings and relations?

I follow Karen Brodkin's (1998) suggestion that it is important to study the articulation between global capitalism, nation-state policies, and race-making processes. I sometimes use the concept of race and sometimes use the concept of ethnicity, because day laborers are singled out in the discourses of the press, agrarian entrepreneurs, informants, and secondary literature by their assumed physical characteristics and by their alleged cultural heritage. I argue that local understandings of "race" and "culture" complement each other to place day laborers in a vulnerable position within Baja Californian society.

The Development of Agribusiness in the San Quintín Valley

San Quintín is located in the Baja Californian peninsula, about 185 miles south of the Mexico–United States border. Agriculture did not prosper in San Quintín before the 1970s because of the scarcity of rainfall and lack of sufficient surface water for irrigation. For the same reasons, the valley has been sparsely populated. Until recently, the dominant form of landowner-ship was the ejido,[6] a public land grant to a particular community given in the context of the post-Revolutionary agrarian reform and in exchange for political support to the state and ruling party (Garduño, García, and Morán 1989; Nugent 1993). According to Mexican agrarian law, ejidos could not be sold or rented.[7] In the mid-1970s, San Quintín became an important center for the production of vegetables and fruits, particularly tomatoes, for ex-port to the United States. This transformation was made possible by the import of advanced Israeli technology that allowed the extraction of water from the subsoil and its efficient use through drip irrigation systems. Once water became available, commercial agriculture boomed; the area enjoys abundant sunshine for most of the year, the soils are very fertile, and it is located in close proximity of the United States. In addition, local producers possessed considerable entrepreneurial know-how learned in previous ex-periences with irrigated commercial agriculture in neighboring areas. Mexican entrepreneurs from Sinaloa and Mexicali have contributed to the transformation of San Quintín into an agro-export emporium (Garduño, García, and Morán 1989; Garduño 1991). Before the 1992 reform that allowed for the privatization of ejidos, agribusiness entrepreneurs rented land ille-gally. Since the reform, a process of concentration of land has taken place (Rhett-Mariscal 1998). For example, the García family, owner of the firm San Vicente Camalú, was able to accumulate more than 45,000 acres of formerly ejidal land by the mid-1990s (*Zeta*, March 26–April 3 1997).[8]

With the development of commercial agriculture, great numbers of laborers were needed. The region was sparsely populated and horticulture required intensive labor; in addition, northern producers sought a labor force that would accept lower wages than would local workers favored by the distribution of ejidos, work opportunities in fisheries, industry, and tourism, and the ease of migration to the United States. Local producers imported Oaxacan day laborers through the enganche system, first from neighboring commercial agriculture areas in Sinaloa, where peasants from the southwest of Mexico had been hired since the 1950s (Garduño 1991), and later directly from their own communities in Oaxaca and Guerrero. When migration patterns were established, southwestern peasants started to arrive and settle in San Quintín on their own. In the 1990s, 16.82 percent of day laborers in northwestern commercial agriculture were enganchados, whereas 83.18 percent had arrived on their own (Sánchez 1994, 31). However, the enganche system remains so important for agrarian entrepreneurs that the co-owner of an important agrarian firm claimed to have traveled personally on several occasions to recruit Mixtecs in Oaxaca (*La Jornada*, July 18, 1996[9]). While I was doing fieldwork in San Quintín, I heard rumors that in times of need, agrarian entrepreneurs sent airplanes to Oaxaca to bring indigenous workers to San Quintín.

Due to the cycle of cultivation of the tomato, a great number of workers are needed only during the harvest from May to August (Garduño, García, and Morán 1989). As Michael Kearney (1988) has noted, the use of a temporary labor force working for wages below the level of reproduction, who therefore need additional sources of income to survive and find them in subsistence agriculture in their communities, is made possible by the articulation of subsistence agriculture in Oaxaca with commercial agriculture in the north of Mexico. Subsistence agriculture secures the reproduction of the labor force when it is not needed by the commercial sector. For example, peasants born and raised in villages are hired in their own communities by representatives of agribusiness entrepreneurs. When day laborers are not needed in the commercial sector because of seasonal fluctuations in the demand for labor or contractions in the market, workers are thrown back onto their village economies (Kearney 1988). Meanwhile, wages earned in commercial agriculture contribute to the maintenance of the subsistence sector. Day laborers periodically send savings to their hometowns to invest in additional land, cattle, or materials that they need to cultivate the land, such as fertilizers and tools. Luis Vazquez León (forthcoming) argues that an increasing number of day laborers are becoming fully proletarianized with the end of what he calls indigenist policies. These include the end of the agrarian reform with the amendment of article 27 of the Mexican constitution, which allows for the privatization of ejidos and puts an end to additional distribution of land, and the reduction of social funding for agencies working in the countryside, like the National Indigenist Institute.

The 1996 San Quintín Riot

Depending on the accounts, between five hundred and one thousand day laborers, some of them indigenous and some mestizo, some from Oaxaca and some from the northern state of Sinaloa, protested to the management of the Santa Anita Ranch on July 3, 1996, because they had not been paid their wages for several weeks.[10] The ranchers called the police to control the protest. After being provoked by the police, who had hit a ten-year-old field worker, day laborers responded, and several policemen were hurt during the disturbances. Protesters burned municipal, state, and federal police cars as well as a ranch-owned truck that had been used to block transpeninsular Highway 1, which crosses Baja California from north to south. Then they occupied and vandalized town offices and looted about twenty-five shops. After the riot, government officials and the press started to pay a great deal of attention to the working and living conditions of indigenous day laborers in the San Quintín Valley. A government official from the National Indianist Institute stated, "Before the looting, San Quintín was an abandoned area. Nobody had ever seen the governor here. After the events, when something happens, a plane arrives directly from Mexicali [the administrative capital of the state of Baja California] (interview by author with INI official, August 1997). The effects of the riot were magnified by widespread fear of an indigenous uprising that would replicate ongoing armed struggles in the southern states of Chiapas and Guerrero.[11]

The Increased Salience of Earnings Under "Flexible Capitalism"

The San Quintín riot started because employers had not paid their workers for several weeks when they were supposed to pay them weekly. Official investigations that took place after the events revealed that local agribusiness often paid workers late, not only on the ranch where the disturbances had taken place but also on other ranches, such as Agrícola Peninsular, a firm from Sinaloa that was often late with payments and was the center of strikes and other disturbances (*Cambio*, September 24, 1996). Anthropologist Víctor Clark stated that day laborers were often paid from three weeks to a month late in most Baja Californian agribusiness (*Cambio*, July 5, 1996). Migrant day laborers stated in interviews that they perceived work in the valley as a temporary sacrifice they made to save enough money to send to their families down south and, ideally, to invest in land or a small business in their hometown. They did not complain as much about terrible working and living conditions, mistreatment, long workdays, or health-related issues. However, they were not willing to accept threats to their earnings, which they perceived as considerable in relation to the wages they received in their region of origin. Don Isaías Vázquez, an indigenous leader in San Quintín, highlighted two protests that took place in 1996. Both of them contested a threat to the earnings of indigenous migrants. The first is the riot analyzed here. The second was a protest organized by Don Isaías himself against a corrupt government official who worked for the telegraph company. Day laborers used the public telegraph to send their savings to their hometown. They complained that their families in Oaxaca were not receiving the whole amount sent, and in some cases not receiving anything at all. An additional grievance was that when they sent money in U.S. dollars, it was not being exchanged at current rates.[12] After some controversy, the corrupt government official was fired (*Mexicano*, December 3, 1996; *Mexicano*, December 16, 1996).

As Steve Striffler (1998) has noted, it is difficult to develop a worker's identity under flexible labor practices that do not secure stable employment and the long-term reproduction of the labor force. In this situation, Striffler argues, workers tend to perceive what they do as temporary, a sacrifice that will allow them to save for something else, such as opening a small business, which becomes their "wishful thinking" identity. This happens even as workers are caught in this "temporary" situation for long periods of time, as indigenous migrants are in San Quintín. Similarly, in a study of export-oriented agriculture in Kenya, Dolan (2002, 668) claims, "It is French bean income, . . . rather than labor, which has become the terrain of overt conflict between husband and wife. In general [Kenyan] women have not openly challenged the intensification of the labour process." Thus, earnings instead of labor conditions, work hours, or health issues become even more central to workers than before. This idea of the understanding of work as temporary and the lack of a solid worker identity has also been found in other sectors typical of flexible capitalism, such as export-oriented industries (Fernández Kelly 1983; Freeman 2000).

Race and Culture as Class

Press accounts describe the protesters as day laborers, agrarian workers, migrant day laborers, indigenous, or Mixtec. These terms are used interchangeably as synonyms in the same press account. Two different discourses are used to represent the protesters: one based on class and the other based on ethnicity.[13] These images mirror the two government institutions working with the same population in the valley: the National Indigenist Institute (INI) and the National Program in Solidarity with Day Laborers [Programa Nacional en Solidaridad con los Jornaleros Agrícolas] (PRONSJAG).[14] The former uses an ethnic approach, whereas the latter promotes a class-based perspective. Dual representations and institutions reflect different ways that popular groups have been incorporated into the Mexican state: as peasants, workers, or popular urban groups (class-based approach), and as Indians (ethnic approach). Different discourses also allow institutions to compete for clients and resources. However, as seen in the press accounts that discuss the riot, class and ethnic terms are used interchangeably. Moreover, both government institutions address the same population.[15] It has been claimed that in the contemporary Mexican context it is possible to understand the term "day laborer" (*jornalero*) as a synonym for "Indian" (Macip 1997; Vázquez León 2003). The word "migrant" is also often used as a euphemism for "Indian" in Baja California.

Despite being represented as homogeneously indigenous, San Quintín's day laborers are a mixture of migrant semiproletarians. Most are from the southwest of Mexico, from the states of Oaxaca and Guerrero, but some are from other regions. Some speak indigenous languages, particularly Mixtec, Zapotec, and Triqui, some identify as Indians, but others neither speak an indigenous language nor identify as indigenous. This situation evokes Karen Brodkin's (1998) suggestion that race can be interpreted in some cases as a relationship to the means of production. According to Brodkin, by performing certain jobs perceived as degraded, workers might become nonwhite. She illustrates this statement with the example of Jewish immigrants in New York City in the early twentieth century, who became nonwhite or "off-white" as they underwent a process of proletarianization and de-skilling. Similarly, migrants in San Quintín, whether they speak an indigenous language or not, are defined as "Indian" when they arrive to work in the fields as day laborers.

Brodkin (1998, 244) argues, "Sometimes state race-making policies have dovetailed with capitalist projects of organizing relationships to the means of production racially." This works as Brodkin says in the case of San Quintín, because a number of state institutions, particularly the National

Indigenist Institute, the Department of Public Education, and the Department of Popular Cultures, encouraged day laborers to organize under ethnic banners and promoted indigenous languages and what state officials understand as indigenous culture. This is important even for those who arrived in San Quintín speaking an indigenous language, because traditionally in post-Revolutionary Mexico, an Indian who left his or her community and learned Spanish was expected to become mestizo/mestiza. Interestingly, some government officials are willing to redefine the meaning of Indian and make it more inclusive when addressing day laborers in the north of Mexico to keep them from assimilating (see chapter 3). For instance, the director of PRONSJAG claimed that only 80 percent of the day laborer population was indigenous in the late 1990s (interview by author, August 1997). In contrast, the anthropologist of INI asserted, "Work in the fields is 100 percent indigenous. Indians have very good characteristics for this kind of work. They are docile people: they are able to endure terrible working conditions without complaint. Besides, they are very cheap labor force" (interview by author, August 1997).

As a consequence of the historical subordination of indigenous people in the colonial and postcolonial periods, they are expected to accept lower wages than mestizos and to work and live in worse conditions. They are also constructed as more docile, patient, and frugal. In the 1990s, San Quintín's field workers were paid between 25 and 35 Mexican pesos a day (between $3 and $4.50 U.S. a day at the going exchange rate), whereas Sinaloan women hired in the packing plants earned approximately 75 pesos a day ($9 U.S.) (Ortiz and Vélez 1992). Employers argue that Indians are used to living in small, crowded rooms without running water or electricity in their region of origin and how they are lodged in San Quintín in employer-provided camps only replicates their traditional way of life (*La Jornada*, July 18, 1996).[16] Meanwhile, mestiza female workers are provided with relatively decent housing with services (Nagengast and Kearney 1990). Not only employers but also representatives from official unions construct Indians as backward and primitive people who do not need basic services. Consequently, official unions don't need to struggle for these facilities. An official union representative claimed, "The temporary day laborer from Oaxaca and Guerrero does not have the culture to keep clean the room that is provided for him. If they get bathrooms, they would still defecate outside. They do not use the showers and, even if they would get a kitchen, they would prefer to use open fires inside the rooms" (*La Jornada*, July 20, 1996).[17] In contrast to this statement, an indigenous woman who worked in San Quintín as an adolescent claimed that her most humiliating experience in the valley was the lack of hygienic facilities that forced her to be dirty while she was working there (interview by author, January 1997).

Employers also exploit regional differences between the north and south. Poor migrants from the south are despised and discriminated against in the north, a region that enjoys higher living standards. Using the contrast between the north and the south, an employer claimed that Oaxacans should not complain about their situation in San Quintín because "in their homeland they live 100 times worse" (*La Jornada*, July 18, 1996).[18] Similarly, the leader of an official union argued that many exaggerate when they refer to the situation of Mixtecs in the San Quintín Valley. They make 35 pesos a day ($4.50 U.S.). "This is much more than what they are able to earn in their homeland, which is about 12 pesos [$1.50 U.S. a day]" (*La Jornada*, July 20, 1996).[19]

The temporary transfer of workers allows employers and authorities to argue that services and infrastructure don't need to be provided or can't be provided for this population in the receiving area, where they are perceived as a transient group (*población flotante*) (interview by author with INI anthropologist, 1997). Thus, their work can be used without the corresponding investment in their reproduction and welfare that is transferred to their region of origin. Although it is often assumed that the entire day laborer population is transient, a large group has settled or would like to settle. About 14,000 day laborers had settled permanently in the valley in the 1990s. Of a sample of 1,800 families, 35 percent wished to settle in San Quintín if they had the opportunity to do so (Garduño 1991). However, the *Program of Regional Development of the San Quintín Valley,* published by the state of Baja California, insists on representing day laborers as a transient population: "Some of these workers settle in town, but the majority travel constantly in a circuit from Oaxaca to Sinaloa to Baja California, because they do not like to separate themselves from their places of origin (Estado de Baja California 1995, 59). Thus, strong Oaxacan (also used in the north as synonymous for "Indian") identity is deployed to portray day laborers as outsiders, and their unstable situation is presented as a choice.

The image of the transient population may transmit the idea that this people are "not quite there." Although employers have deliberately sought to hire these migrant workers, scholars, the press, and middle-class Baja Californians often represent indigenous migrants as people escaping poverty (Velasco 1995; Garduño 1991). When I was doing fieldwork, I heard rumors of a proposal suggesting that the state of Oaxaca should subsidize the state of Baja California for accepting this population.

The rationale used by producers to account for the segmentation of the labor force is based on assumed physical features and cultural traits. Sinaloan women are believed to be cleaner than indigenous workers and therefore better suited for packing tasks. A newspaper reported, "The Magaña family owns packing plants of tomato and cucumber. There, they only hire young women and men from Sinaloa. Producers claim, "In the packing plants you need hygienic people. We can't use the Mixtecs for that job" (La Jornada, July 18, 1996).[20] It is interesting that day laborers are not allowed to become more "hygienic," given the lack of basic services in employer-provided camps. Producers also argue that Sinaloan workers are taller and can better reach the packing belts (Garduño 1991). However, observers have pointed out that Sinaloan women often use platforms or benches to reach the belts. Producers deploy a similar idea to justify the assignment of indigenous workers to the fields to perform the harshest and worst-paid tasks. They argue that indigenous people are short and, therefore, closer to earth. Thus, they are better endowed to work the land than taller mestizo people (La Jornada, July 18, 1996).[21]

Poor hygiene and short height are characteristics associated with being Indian in the north of Mexico. Dirt and impurity are features universally assigned to subordinate groups. As Mary Douglas (1966) has noted, ideas of purity and impurity reflect notions of the social order and social hierarchies. The belief that subordinate groups are impure contributes to keeping them segregated and marginalized, as in the case discussed here. Differences in height are also used to distinguish southerners from northerners. In a conference on racism and daily life, a Mixtec teacher and leader argued that Indians were discriminated against in the north because they were dark and short (chaparros), "We give preference to those who are tall, to those who are white," he said (Montiel, speech delivered at COLEF conference, October 1996). Sinaloan women, in contrast, are locally constructed as white, tall, and beautiful. Differences in height between northerners and southerners are not only discursive marks; they are real physical effects of social inequalities that allow differential access to a diet rich in proteins and nutrients. The north has historically been a cattle-raising economy, and even people of modest means have been able to consume more protein than in the south. In this case, social inequalities and their physical effects (differences in height) are associated with regional contrasts.

Day laborers do not enjoy job security. Their employers consider them temporary workers despite the fact that some of them have been working for the same employer for up to ten years (Garduño 1991). Their workday lasts for ten, eleven, or more hours. In busy periods, they work seven days a week without getting double pay for the seventh day as Mexican law requires. Nor do employers pay day laborers for their lunch hour or for the vacation time that corresponds to the time worked (Garduño 1991; INI 1997). These benefits are not denied, on the other hand, to permanent workers in charge of management or mechanized jobs or to temporary workers in the packing plants (Sánchez 1994; Garduño 1991).

Most illnesses and deaths among day laborers are caused by a combination of malnutrition, lack of hygiene, lack of protection from weather conditions, and exposure to dangerous chemicals and pesticides. Lack of adequate medical attention combines with harsh living conditions to account for the poor health and high mortality rate among day laborer families. Because many day laborers are seasonal workers, employers get medical passes, which they are supposed to make available to workers upon request. The worker needs to show the pass at the public hospital to be received. Because farmers underreport the number of workers that they employ to avoid paying social security, most of the time there are not enough medical passes for all the workers (Garduño, García, and Morán 1989; Sánchez 1994). Moreover, the allocation of medical passes to the employer, and not to the worker, provides the former with an additional source of power over the latter. Public medical attention that should be a worker's right according to Mexican labor law becomes a *patrón*'s favor. In addition, indigenous workers are discriminated against when they try to use public medical services (interview by author with INI official, 1997).

In spite of this situation, the *Program for Regional Development of the*

San Quintín Valley states, "We have to realize that Mixtec migrants do not trust conventional medicine and, therefore, they are reluctant to use the services that health institutions offer to them because many of them prefer the methods and customs of their indigenous ancestors" (Estado de Baja California 1995, 61). This claim should be contrasted with the fact that day laborer unions have been struggling for years to get a public hospital in the San Quintín area (*La Jornada*, January 19 1997;[22] *Cambio*, January 18 1997).[23] A young woman who works as day laborer stated, "We, the poor, do not have access to health care. Therefore, we have to treat ourselves with whatever we have: our teas and our egg massages" (interview by author, January 1997). I do not mean that indigenous day laborers do not respect their own traditional health practices. They do not, however, see a contradiction between preserving their health customs and having access to Western medicine, or, perhaps, as the woman quoted previously notes, they understand their own health care practices in the context of their lack of access to another system that they perceive as more efficient in the face of illness and death. In this case, the "culture" of day laborers as defined by municipal government officials is used to justify their exclusion from a basic service despite day laborers' desperate attempts to make themselves heard. Their lack of access to health services, an effect of poverty, is constructed as a cultural choice: they like it that way. Municipal government officials pretend to be sensitive toward indigenous workers when in fact they are silencing their voice.

Child Labor and the Peasant Family as a Unit of Production in Commercial Agriculture

According to participants in the 1996 San Quintín protest, violence started when the police hit a ten-year-old fieldworker. Violence against a child-worker not only seemed unjustified but also symbolized the daily use of children as adults in the farms. A newspaper account noted that many protesters were working children. Twenty out of sixty-four people detained by the police after the riot were minors (*Cambio*, July 5, 1996). About one-third of all workers in commercial agriculture in the north of Mexico are children under the age of fourteen, the minimum age to work according to Mexican law. Children begin to work between the ages of six and nine. At the age of nine, they are considered regular workers. Children perform special tasks such as distributing water and killing small rodents that damage the plants. "Weeding is the activity in which child labor is most often used because it does not require physical strength, but it does require small and dexterous hands and a worker able to squat for long hours" (Sánchez 1994, 13). At the time of the harvest, children fill their buckets with tomatoes as adults. Day laborers ensure that children are paid the same amount as adults (interviews by author, 1997). Because children work as adults, and because many are migrant workers, it is very difficult for them to attend school, which further limits their chances for social mobility. When I was doing fieldwork, the Program in Solidarity with Day Laborers was experimenting with a school system adapted to the needs of day laborer children. This experience was financed by the Inter-American Development Bank, which invested $5.6 million for day care and education in the San Quintín area (Vázquez León 2003). However, it was difficult for the program to succeed, given the situation in which these children live. Moreover, classrooms were small and were located in the barracks where day laborers live. The barracks did not have windows, lacked adequate illumination, and were extremely hot and uncomfortable in the summer because the heat was concentrated by the tin plates out of which they were built.

Some scholars working for the Mexican state perceive child labor as an indigenous tradition. Millán and Rubio (1992, 11) state, "Indigenous children wander the city working with their parents or begging. This problem is particularly delicate . . . because the ethnic and cultural characteristics of migrants require the integration of children to the family's economy." Again, an effect of economic deprivation is characterized as part of indigenous culture. Other government officials claim that since child labor is not going to disappear, the government should regulate it. "The working child does not exist in legislation, which allows for more irregularities" (interview by author with INI official, August 1997). However, the regulation of child labor would mean the official recognition of a situation in which many children are deprived of an education, a healthy childhood, and the possibility for social mobility.

One explanation for the high number of children working in commercial agriculture in the north of Mexico is that whole families are hired. Given low wages and high prices, the only way for day laborers to save money to send home (their main purpose for coming to San Quintín) is to have many family members working at the same time. As Sánchez (1994) has noted, the family is a key element in commercial agriculture in the north of Mexico. Families work together in the same group (*cuadrilla*), divide tasks among themselves, and help each other. Keeping the family together improves the productivity of individual workers. If a family member is unable to fulfill the quotas assigned to him or her, the rest of the family works extra to achieve set goals. Both employers and workers agree on the convenience of hiring whole families and having them work together. Mexican commercial agriculture, thus, does not proletarianize peasants as individuals. On the contrary, it keeps the peasant family and its mechanisms of self-exploitation intact because employers (and workers) perceive it as profitable. Similarly, Dolan (2002, 661) argues for the case of export agriculture in Kenya, "Companies remunerate growers on the basis of the unit of produce harvested regardless of labor input, thereby banking on the process of family self-exploitation to meet production objectives. Export firms thus harness an entire family to global agricultural production, trusting that the labor process will be managed through cultural norms of rights and responsibilities." The organization of workers in families also makes the labor force more flexible. When there is a high demand for labor, everybody works long hours, seven days a week. "When the market shrinks, which often happens with vegetables, only two or three days of work are required. In those cases, women and children are the first to be laid off" (Sánchez 1994, 10).

"Passive, Innocent" Indian Protesters and the "Outside Agitator" Thesis

Although day laborers were well organized into a number of independent and official unions,[24] no organization claimed responsibility for the protest of the Santa Anita Ranch, perhaps for fear of retribution. Although the events were relatively violent, most press accounts did not convey a threatening image of day laborers. Instead, the laborers were represented as peaceful people and as victims of exploitation by local *caciques* (agrarian entrepreneurs) and desertion by government authorities. Journalists and invited writers, reflecting on the riot, recognized the terrible conditions of

Who are the so-called Ensenada[36] caciques? How was this class of entrepreneurs formed? In the 1990s, fourteen large and medium-sized enterprises belonging to Mexican families concentrated most of the San Quintín Valley's production. Mexican entrepreneurs sometimes contract their production with transnational firms and sometimes they export directly. When they work by contract, local producers provide land, labor, and labor management. Corporations supply seeds, fertilizer, technology, and technological advice and participate in production decisions. Not all the production of the San Quintín Valley is exported, however. Top-quality products are exported, whereas products that do not reach quality standards are sold in the Mexican market. Some Mexican firms, such as Los Pinos, export directly to the U.S. market. They own a number of trailers for the transportation of tomatoes and have a subsidiary firm in the United States called Los Pinos Enterprises (Ortiz and Vélez 1992). In 1996, the Mexican government negotiated tomato exports within the context of the North American Free Trade Agreement (NAFTA). Producers of tomatoes from Florida accused Mexican tomato producers of dumping because they were allegedly selling the product below market price. This action was feasible because of the low wages and poor conditions offered to agricultural workers in the north of Mexico (*Cambio*, July 11, 1996). Although the agro-export business benefits both Mexican producers and transnational corporations, it is often rumored that Mexican producers are only "straw men" for foreign interests (*prestanombres*), or even that foreign interests operate directly in San Quintín. This allows for the formulation of nationalist arguments against foreign agribusiness. It also liberates Mexicans from responsibility for the exploitation of indigenous workers and the environment. In San Quintín, however, everybody knows the most powerful families of Mexican farmers and their growing prosperity. William Rhett-Mariscal (1998, 26) notes, "The major producers in the valley control all aspects of production—from seed development, crop farming and harvesting to packing, transportation, and marketing in the U.S." San Quintín's producers are organized in associations such as the Association of Producers of Camalú, the Association of Producers of Colonia Vicente Guerrero, and the Association of Producers of the San Quintín Valley, which represent them and defend their interests vis-à-vis the state and popular groups

(INI 1997). The producers' neighborhood, "an area of luxurious modern houses built in American style" (Ortiz and Vélez 1992), contrasts with the miserable living quarters of indigenous workers.

San Quintín's producers are often accused of breaking agrarian, labor, and environmental laws (Garduño 1991; Ortiz and Vélez 1992). According to Garduño, producers use twice as much water as is naturally replaced in underground deposits and, in the presence of workers, including children and pregnant women who are then exposed to these chemicals, use spray fertilizers and pesticides that are forbidden in the United States. There is a great deal of confusion in San Quintín regarding cultivated area, production, and labor statistics. Producers tend to underestimate cultivated area to avoid accusations of exploiting water resources and to reduce payment of social security, taxes, and other obligations (Garduño 1991; Ortiz and Vélez 1992). However, it is well known that commercial agriculture is quite prosperous in the valley. Some studies claim that the cultivated area increased from about 10,000 acres to approximately 22,000 during the 1990s, reaching the maximum that can be cultivated given available water resources (INI 1997). The production rate of tomatoes per hectare is the highest in Mexico, doubling the national rate. In the 1990s, Baja California became the second-ranking state in Mexico in the export of vegetables, accounting for 12 percent of the total exported.

The analysis that follows summarizes the interpretations of the situation in San Quintín as they appeared in the Baja Californian newspapers *Mexicano, Cambio,* and *Zeta* and in the national newspaper *La Jornada* from the day of the riot, July 3, to December 1996. For several months after the riots, journalists and invited writers reflected on the causes and consequences of the indigenous protest. Some journalists interpret the situation of exploitation of indigenous workers by a Mexican entrepreneur group through the image of the "region of refuge" (Aguirre Beltrán 1967)—the isolated region ruled by a ruthless rural aristocracy where the revolutionary state does not yet penetrate. They criticize the violence and abuse of armed *patrones* as well as the abandonment of the authorities (see, for example, *Mexicano,* July 6 1996; *Cambio,* July 7 1996).[37] This image is paradoxical in Baja California, a dynamic region neighboring the United States that uses sophisticated technology to produce food and industrial items for export.

The journalists exploit this paradox. They see a contrast between the concept of caciquismo, understood as a leftover from the pre-Revolutionary past, and the modern reality of Baja California (*Cambio*, July 11, 1996).[38] This tradition/modernity paradox is one of the important points of the debate.

Whereas some journalists write about caciques, others focus on the transnational companies that are siphoning off national wealth through the use of Mexican "straw men." Lozoya, a journalist, writes, "The capital that is used there (San Quintín) to allow for agrarian production arrives from the United States, which is the country that makes business profits out of San Quintín's agriculture and where our products are exported. An infinitely smaller portion of the profits stays in the hands of Mexican straw men [*prestanombres*] and corrupt authorities who let the abuses continue" (*Cambio*, May 4 1996).[39] Journalists argue that transnational companies commit injustices against indigenous peasants and encourage the appearance of guerrilla groups, such as those operating in Chiapas and Guerrero (*Mexicano*, July 5, 1996). The press rarely perceives or expresses the connection between Mexican caciques and transnational companies that characterizes contract agriculture; either one side or the other is emphasized. Perhaps this connection is not made because government officials, activists, scholars, and others who influence public opinion interpret contemporary contract agriculture through 1970s conceptualizations of either caciquismo or imperialism.

Two separate discourses interpret injustice in the San Quintín Valley. One understands San Quintín's problems in terms of regional "tradition" versus national "modernity." Landowners exploit indigenous peasants by extralegal means. The mission of the post-Revolutionary state, according to this interpretation, is to redeem indigenous peasants from the power of regional caciques and to "modernize" social relations at the regional level. This resonates with the idea that San Quintín is an area abandoned or deserted by the authorities (interview by author with INI official, August 1997). This discourse builds on an influential tradition of Mexican scholarship that originates in the late 1960s and 1970s. For example, *Regiones de refugio* by Gonzalo Aguirre Beltrán (1967) and "Classes, Colonialism, and Acculturation" by Rodolfo Stavenhagen (1970) interpret the exploitation of indigenous peasants by mestizo hacendados as a leftover from the colonial past. According to these two authors, the penetration of the revolutionary state into isolated regions will dissolve castelike social relations and will produce "modern" class-based ones.[40]

Another discourse seeking to understand San Quintín's reality criticizes the transition from a nationalist post-Revolutionary to a neoliberal model in which foreign interests take advantage of Mexico's resources. Paradoxically, the transition to neoliberalism is also interpreted with reference to the past, particularly the late nineteenth century Porfiriato, a period characterized by the expansion of capitalism and the penetration of foreign capital into Mexico. An article in the national newspaper *La Jornada* (July 17, 1996)[41] argues, "The work and social conditions are not very different from those prevalent before the 1910 Revolution: long workdays for entire indigenous families brought from the Oaxacan Mixteca, children six years old or younger employed in the harsh jobs of seed-time and harvest, surveyed by private armed security guards in closed ranches. They live in barracks without electricity, drinking water, or bathrooms."

An editorial article written by Tonatiuh Guillén (*Cambio*, July 11, 1996)[42] elaborates on these ideas. Guillén argues that rural caciques used the police illegally to repress workers who were protesting for their legitimate rights. He shows surprise because the events did not happen in a marginal region outside the realm of law such as Chiapas (the "region of refuge" par excellence), but in modern Baja California, the first state in Mexico to have fair elections and to be democratically ruled by the opposition. Guillén is also surprised because the events took place in a rural area characterized by sophisticated technology and export orientation. Baja California's evident "modernity," however, was not reflected, according to the author, in the respect for the citizenship rights of its indigenous workers. Guillén thus contrasts the modernity of Baja California as expressed in globalization, technology, and political tolerance with practices understood as traditional, such as the exercise of arbitrary power by landowners against indigenous people and the lack of respect for workers' rights. The author understands modernity normatively as progress toward the greater democratization of Mexican society. However, he notices that modernity in Baja California has not entailed citizenship rights, which leads him to question recent strategies for development.

San Quintín's reality can be interpreted differently from a regional standpoint. Francisco Vargas reflects on the apparent paradox of the coexistence of traditional and modern traits in Baja California (*Cambio,* July 7, 1996).[43] He argues that modern traits are inherent in the nature of Baja California, whereas traditional features are imported from the south of Mexico. According to the author, companies that have been operating for a longer time in Baja California are not plagued by labor problems. Newly established companies are confronting labor unrest because they try to import to Baja California labor systems that entail levels of exploitation typical of other regions of Mexico. Social conflicts are also imported with indigenous workers from the south of Mexico. The author is using the frontier myth to represent the north of Mexico as a democratic land of opportunity for hardworking, self-made men (Alonso 1995). This image is contrasted with the south, which is perceived as an area characterized by marked social and racial inequalities inherited from an aristocratic colonial past (León Portilla 1972). This approach is typical of northern regionalists who complain about the "invasion" of the north by *chilangos,* a derogatory term for upper- and middle-class people from Mexico City who arrive with capital and expertise and are perceived as arrogant. Northerners also complain about the "invasion" of the north by poor nonwhite southerners who allegedly create social problems.

Indigenous day laborers seem to have internalized this regionalist discourse. Don Isaías Vázquez explained that there was no need for an indigenous guerrilla in Baja California because "Here, the patrones are not caciques like in the south" (interview by author with I. Vázquez, August 1997). This understanding contrasts sharply with the conditions of exploitation that Mixtec workers endure in San Quintín.

It is interesting that the journalists who reflect on the riot represent the region in different ways in relation to the modernity/tradition opposition. A center shaped by the revolutionary state diffuses modernity understood as social justice to regions that are depositories of tradition understood as colonial leftovers and ruthless caste-based exploitation. The second version holds that a modern, dynamic, and democratic frontier north is "invaded" by a hierarchical traditional south. Significantly, in both discourses, tradition is associated with racial discrimination of colonial origin and modernity with greater democratization. The first discourse originates in the center. It is often used by federal government agents (interview by author with INI official, August 1997), whereas the second originates in the region and is used by northern regionalist middle classes. The consensus that modernity means social justice and greater democracy contrasts with the modern caste-based exploitation that takes place in San Quintín.

Conclusion

I have shown how race, culture, and region are used in the San Quintín Valley to reduce labor costs by hiring cheaper workers from the south and by labeling them and maintaining them indigenous to keep them cheap. The Mexican state promotes the preservation of indigenous languages and what government officials understand by indigenous culture in the valley. Meanwhile, some cultural traits, such as hygiene[44] or attachment to traditional indigenous health practices, are used to marginalize indigenous people in the labor market (people who are assumed not to be hygienic are excluded from better paid positions) or deny them necessary services (indigenous day laborers do not need health care because they prefer their own ancestral practices). Furthermore, indigenous migrants are defined as outsiders in Baja California through the idea that they constitute a transient population, which serves to justify denying them the rights enjoyed by locals. Therefore, ideas of race and culture complement each other to place migrant day laborers in a subordinate position in Baja Californian society.

Unequal racial and social relations of colonial origin are reproduced in a contemporary context of high-tech commercial agriculture for export at an international border. Economic modernization, articulation to world markets, and migration to dynamic regions are not bringing about the end of castelike exploitation as Mexican anthropologists of the 1960s and 1970s predicted (Aguirre Beltrán 1967; Stavenhagen 1970). Nagengast and Kearney (1990), Laura Velasco (2002), and others have suggested that day laborers are better equipped to struggle against capitalist and state exploitation when they identify and organize around an indigenous identity. However, I agree with Vázquez León (2003) that we need to examine carefully the disadvantageous consequences for workers of stronger Indian identification. Lower wages, harsher working conditions, and lack of services are still justified in the Mexican context as long as workers are labeled indigenous. It is possible, however, that this association between Indianness and socioeconomic vulnerability will be transformed by multicultural policies in the future.

Scholars working on contract farming of nontraditional agro-exports highlight how "flexible" capitalism transforms local power relations. Michael Watts (1992) has focused on how contract farming has transformed social relations in a West African society despite that transnational companies do not organize production directly. Similarly, Catherine Dolan (2002, 677) discusses how French bean production for export to Europe has "deepened gendered conflicts over labour, land and income" in Kenya. Unlike these interpretations, I argue that contract farming has not transformed but has used traditional social relations arising from a colonial and postcolonial past that has subordinated indigenous populations to non-Indians in the north of Mexico. Thus, an additional benefit accrues for transnational companies when using local partners: they can profit from levels of exploitation that would seem unacceptable in their countries of origin without being directly responsible for them.[45] On the one hand, we could call this process an "externalization of the internal" as Striffler (2002) would have it, because local social relations of colonial origin allow for lower local wages that make the product, in this case tomatoes, more competitive in global markets and may contribute to depressing agricultural wages at a global level. On the other hand, regional social relations are transformed by global contract agriculture in San Quintín, as southern workers are brought to the north of Mexico, where historical ethnic and regional differences are used to lower labor costs. The contrast between the cases studied by Watts (1992) and Dolan (2002) and the case discussed here supports one of the main points that William Roseberry (1989, 1995) emphasizes: similar global processes can produce different results as they interact with diverse histories and sets of social relations.

Given the use of historical inequalities by modern global agriculture, it is only logical that Baja Californians and other Mexicans understand what is happening in San Quintín today in relation to the past. The question of ethnic exploitation and its relationship to modernity takes an interesting twist in the debate over the 1996 San Quintín riot. The debate illuminates an ethic consensus: modernity is still perceived in Mexico as greater social justice because, as Collier and Quaratiello (1994) have noted, the 1910 Revolution is conceptualized not as an event but as an unfinished process that is projected into the future. Paradoxically, castelike exploitation and foreign investment typical of "flexible capitalism" are associated with the past at a moment when neoliberal reforms have halted the revolutionary project.

The literature on globalization analyzes the use of vulnerable groups of workers in assembly industries, export-oriented agriculture, and transnational services. This literature has focused mainly on the feminization of labor as a factor of vulnerability (Dolan 2002; Fernández-Kelly 1983; Freeman 2000; Safa 1995; Striffler 1998; Thrupp 1995). In San Quintín, ethnicity is a key factor of vulnerability, although gender and age are also exploited by agribusiness. As Karen Brodkin (1998) has suggested, more research is needed on the articulation between race and global capitalism.

In the press debate after the riot, indigenous migrants are represented as passive victims. This representation makes invisible the history of activism on the part of indigenous day laborers in the San Quintín Valley and contrasts with a latent fear of Indians, perhaps triggered by a deep feeling of guilt. The image of the passive innocent Indian originates in colonial constructions of Indians as minors who must be represented by a mestizo advocate in legislation and daily practices. Passivity goes hand in hand with the stereotype that indigenous workers are not only frugal (which justifies lower salaries) but also docile. Docility is an important trait assigned to vulnerable groups of workers who become the preferred labor force under neoliberal globalization (Fernández-Kelly 1983; Freeman 2000; Safa 1995; Thrupp 1995). On occasion, indigenous peoples themselves internalize these discourses or use them for their own purposes, such as when they claim to be innocent and passive for fear of repression and of being disqualified as legitimate interlocutors. By accepting dominant discourses about themselves, day laborers make their own activism invisible and allow others to represent them as less than human. Moreover, non-Indians think of indigenous people as either noble savages or irrational beings who would only be capable of agency under the physical effects of hunger or alcohol. This study shows that these images that originated in the colonial past are still pervasive in a context of migration and modernization.

Noticeable in this debate is the contrast between discourses and practices in Baja California—or, more specifically, between populist discourses and practices and capitalist practices (and discourses?). As we have seen, the dominant discourse, the ethical consensus, is very radical compared with other contexts. Most authors support workers against employers and the state. Workers are represented as victims of exploitation and abandonment. They are never represented as violent or evil, nor, except perhaps by local and state authorities, are the employers represented as beneficial investors who provide jobs. Moreover, the state is conceptualized as a mediator between social groups and a champion for the poor and the vulnerable. Paradoxically, this radical discourse coexists with practices that favor businessmen and that don't even guarantee a minimum respect for workers' rights—a respect that is guaranteed in other contexts where dominant discourses may be much less radical.

3

▶▶▶▶▶▶▶▶▶▶▶▶ ◀◀◀◀◀◀◀◀◀◀◀◀

"We Are Against the Government, Although We Are the Government"

State Institutions and Indigenous Migrants in Baja California in the 1990s

Introduction

This chapter explores the role of three state institutions—Instituto Nacional Indigenista (INI) [National Indigenist Institute], Dirección General de Educación Indígena de la Secretaría de Educación Pública (DGEI-SEP) [General Directorate of Indigenous Education of the Department of Public Education], and Dirección General de Culturas Populares [Department of Popular Cultures]—in strengthening indigenous identity and social organization in Baja California during the second half of the 1990s. Unlike other cases, in which states tend to repress difference or tolerate it only when forced to by social movements or international pressures, and in which ethnic movements challenge states, government officials from these Baja Californian state institutions did not perceive the national and the ethnic projects as contradictory. On the contrary, they firmly believed that to promote indigenous identity and social organization was to work for the Mexican nation. As Asad (1993, 17) has argued,

> The claim of many radical critics that hegemonic power necessarily suppresses difference in favor of unity is quite mistaken. Just as mistaken is their claim that power always abhors ambiguity. To secure its unity—to make its own history—dominant power has worked best through differentiating and classifying practices. . . . In this context, power is constructive, not repressive. Furthermore, its ability to select (or construct) the differences that serve its pur-

poses has depended on its exploiting the dangers and opportunities contained in ambiguous situations.

Influential scholars have described the relationship between states and indigenous peoples in Latin America since the nineteenth century and during most of the twentieth century as a conflict in which states tried to impose homogenizing national projects on indigenous peoples that resisted these attempts, reinforcing their consciousness in the process (see, for example, Díaz Polanco 1997; Kearney 1991; Stavenhagen 1994, 2002; Stephen 1996, 2002; Urban and Sherzer 1992; Van Cott 1994; Varese 1996; Warren and Jackson 2002). In the 1990s, a number of Latin American states subscribed to International Labor Organization Convention 169 on the rights of indigenous peoples and reformed their constitutions accordingly, stating that they were willing to recognize and promote indigenous languages, cultures, and forms of social organization (Sieder 2002; Van Cott 2002). This shift has been interpreted as an insufficient and poorly implemented concession made to a growing indigenous movement of continental proportions (Díaz Polanco 1997; Stavenhagen 1994, 2002; Van Cott 1994, 2000; Warren and Jackson 2002). It has also been called a populist initiative intended to overcome a deep crisis of legitimacy and governability in the context of neoliberal reforms that have negatively affected indigenous peoples and other popular groups (Sieder 2002; Stephen 2002; Van Cott 2002); or a response to international pressures (Warren and Jackson 2002). On a more general note, scholars have suggested that the state has been forced to accommodate difference within its institutional system to avoid potentially destructive ethnic conflicts (Maybury-Lewis 1997). In all these cases, the state is imposing homogeneity or responding, tolerating, or accommodating to pressures from below and above.

In the same way, the dominant interpretation of Mexican indigenism—social science based on a sympathetic awareness of the Indian and of public policy toward Indians—holds that from the 1920s to the 1970s, this movement basically consisted of ideas and policies geared toward the assimilation of ethnic groups (Bonfil Batalla 1990; Díaz Polanco 1997; Dietz 1995; Stephen 1997, 2002). A later phase, the so-called new or participatory indigenism that started in the 1970s and promotes the preservation of indigenous cultures and social institutions, is interpreted by critics as a populist discourse with no real impact on indigenist practice (Dietz 1995) or as an "effort to co-opt some indigenous leaders and organizations into government-aligned and funded indigenous organizations and support institutions" (Stephen 1997, 17). Other authors are more optimistic and see a real break with the assimilation of the past that reflects the recent democratization of Mexican society (Hernández Castillo 2001). Still others see a deeper shift toward the celebration of difference in response to internal and external pressures (de la Peña 2002).

While acknowledging the assimilationist tendencies of the Mexican state, other scholars have also noted the tension between these assimilation policies and the historical role of the Mexican state in the reproduction of ethnic differences. Judith Friedlander (1975) argues that the post-Revolutionary Mexican state attempted to integrate Indians into the nation and capitalist development while marking them as different and subordinate, particularly through the school system. George Collier (1994) explores the use of ethnicity by the state and the Partido Revolucionario Institucional to create networks of clients. Although in several publications Michael Kearney (1988, 1991, 1996a) has understood the Mexican state as an agent of homogenization, he has also acknowledged that nation-states promote contradictory projects that seek cultural homogeneity while favoring the reproduction of ethnic differences on which the class system relies (1996b). Similarly, in a recent book entitled *Race and Nation in Modern Latin America*, Applebaum, Macpherson and Rosemblatt claim that nation building was not simply a homogenizing process based on the eradication of difference, although sometimes it worked that way, "Though elites advocated a process of cultural homogenization that, given prevalent cultural definitions of race, implied racial whitening, they maintained the racial distinctions that undergirded efforts to stratify and control labor" (2003, 6).

Building on these insights, I explore the role of some Baja Californian government institutions in the reproduction of ethnic boundaries and the complex effects of neoindigenist policies. I will focus on three questions: What did indigenous identity, culture, and social organization mean for Baja Californian government officials in the late 1990s? What were state agencies doing to preserve or reinforce these and to convince citizens to adopt and internalize official constructions of ethnicity? What could be the intended or unintended consequences of these policies in the context of Baja California?

In this chapter, I have included individualized narratives about government officials and their points of view, as well as the specific histories and approaches of particular state institutions, in order to show that the state is not an impersonal entity and to avoid reifying the state. Individuals working for the state are not free to act as they wish, but they do apply wider state projects, if these exist, which is also an empirical question, adapting them to their own personal philosophies as well as to regional contexts. I find inspiration in the insights of *The Great Arch: English State Formation as Cultural Revolution* by Corrigan and Sayer (1985), *Everyday Forms of State Formation* by Joseph and Nugent (1994), and other recent publications on the anthropology of the state. Corrigan and Sayer argue that acceptable forms of social identity are created, spread, and naturalized through state laws, institutions, administrative procedures, and government rituals. I show how official definitions of ethnicity are spread, and to a certain degree internalized by subjects, through schooling, labeling by some state institutions, distribution of resources to those who adopt state-sanctioned forms of identity, and state-sponsored social organization. *The Great Arch* also inquires into the connections between the cultural changes that state formation brings about—among them the promotion of officially sanctioned identities and other forms of moral regulation—and the development of capitalism in England. According to the authors, state-sponsored cultural transformations are both necessary for the development of capitalism and somewhat independent from socioeconomic processes and relations. I look here at the complex and sometimes contradictory connections between the creation and diffusion of official identities and capitalist interests in the north of Mexico.

Fernando Coronil (1997) carries out an interesting analysis of the relationship between the Venezuelan state and capitalists at both the national and international levels. He describes the relationships of state institutions and national projects to national and international businessmen and companies and shows with great detail that both the state and the national bourgeoisie, despite their considerable power based on oil income, are ultimately subject to international capital and its logic. Steve Striffler has also effectively analyzed the workings of state and capital by looking at the actions of particular individuals and organizations. The vivid detail with which Coronil and Striffler make their points, avoiding the reification of state and capital, is an inspiration for this chapter. Unlike Coronil, who focuses on the connections between the state and elites, this chapter highlights the relationship of the state with marginal groups.

Joseph and Nugent emphasize the importance of looking at regional and historical variations of state formation. Following this suggestion, this chapter shows that the Mexican state and its projects are not monolithic. On the contrary, Mexican state institutions have been characterized by a diversity of tendencies that reflect institutional as well as regional heterogeneity. Finally, William Roseberry (1994) emphasizes that popular groups do not necessarily accept or reproduce uncritically official discourses and imposed identities, although these come to constitute their meaningful framework of discourse and agency. Like Roseberry, I look at how popular groups sometimes accommodate themselves to official identities and sometimes contest them or use them selectively for their own purposes in an ambivalent manner.

Mexican Indigenism: Assimilation of Indigenous People or Reproduction of Ethnic Differences?

Indigenism, understood as a sympathetic awareness of the Indian by non-Indian intellectuals (Stabb 1959) and as a compromise between social science and public policy (Dietz 1995), has a long history in Mexico. It has its origins in the colonial period, when intellectuals such as the Jesuit Francisco Clavijero studied the pre-Hispanic past as a means of celebrating the classic roots of American civilization (Dawson 1998). After independence, elites who wished to create a national identity distinct from Spain used ancient Indian civilizations as symbols of the Mexican nation. At the same time, nineteenth-century elites emphasized their own European roots and despised contemporary Indians, blacks, and *castas* (mixed bloods) in order to differentiate themselves from the masses (Dietz 1995). This tension between the romantic glorification of the Indian past and the dismissal of contemporary indigenous people has been reproduced to a certain extent by post-Revolutionary regimes and lasts to this day (Dietz 1995).

Mexican indigenism reached maturity after the 1910 Revolution but retained some of its nineteenth-century characteristics, such as its relationship to nation building. Progressive intellectuals and social reformers concerned with the lot of Indians reached positions of power in post-Revolutionary governments, refined the tradition of non-Indian thought about the Indian, and became involved in the design of public policies. Indigenism was institutionalized as early as 1917 with the creation of the Dirección de Antropología [Direction of Anthropology] and other state institutions that addressed the Indian question (Dawson 1998). This process of institutionalization was enhanced in the 1940s with the founding, among other institutions and programs, of the Instituto Nacional Indigenista in 1948. INI's original function was to coordinate the activities of different state institutions in indigenous regions.

Critical scholars have interpreted classical indigenism (1917–1970) as an instrument the post-Revolutionary state used to homogenize the Mexican population. These authors argue that indigenism's goal has been to teach Indian populations the Spanish language and Western ways in order to integrate them into capitalist development (Bonfil Batalla 1990; Díaz Polanco 1997; Stavenhagen 1994). In other words, critics argue that indigenism has understood ethnic difference as an obstacle for the consolidation of the nation and that it has promoted racial and cultural mixing (Dietz 1995). The impact of classical indigenism, however, has been more complex than this interpretation allows. Although indigenism did aim to assimilate indigenous people, some of its ideas and practices caused the reinforcement of ethnic differences.

The founders of revolutionary indigenism, Manuel Gamio and Moisés Sáenz among others, aimed to incorporate Indians into Western culture and national society. Inspired by anthropologist Franz Boas, with whom some of them had studied or worked, *indigenistas* did not believe in the biological inferiority of indigenous peoples, which was a progressive position at a time when biological racism was still dominant. However, they thought that, as a result of colonial oppression, indigenous cultures had become impoverished and were themselves contributing to the marginalization of indigenous populations. Thus, they believed that Indians needed to learn Spanish and adopt Western values to move up the socioeconomic ladder. The process of assimilation, according to early revolutionary indigenistas, should rely less on the repressive methods of the nineteenth century, such as the use of the military and the prohibition against the use of indigenous languages and dress, and more on nonrepressive methods, such as education policies (Dietz 1995). Gamio took charge of the Dirección de Antropología that was part of the Department of Agriculture.[1] From this institution he started an ambitious research project intended to provide a scientific basis for assimilation policies. Moisés Sáenz focused on education as the tool for the integration and development of indigenous populations. With the creation of indigenous boarding schools, rural elementary schools, and cultural missions, Sáenz transformed the Department of Public Education into a key institution in indigenous regions (Dietz 1995).

Despite their commitment to integration, pioneer indigenistas like Gamio and Sáenz started a project that contributed a great deal to the continuation of ethnic differences. They encouraged pioneer research on Mexico's pre-Hispanic civilizations and contemporary indigenous cultures that provided a symbolic foundation for Mexican nationalism. A body of knowledge that constructed Indian and mestizo Mexico as essentially different began to build up. The very existence of this body of knowledge, as well as of public institutions and professionals specifically concerned with Indians, had a considerable impact on the reinforcement of ethnic boundaries, as these professionals and institutions were likely to invent and reinvent their own subjects of study. In the same landscapes in which American and European researchers such as Robert Redfield (1930), Oscar Lewis (1951), and George Foster (1967) found peasants or the Mexican "folk," Mexican anthropologists such as Alfonso Villa Rojas (1955), who worked with Redfield and Malinowski, found Indians who spoke unfamiliar languages and wore exotic costumes. Interestingly, Mexican peasants seemed more alien in the writings of some Mexican intellectuals than in those of foreigners.

Mexican indigenistas contributed to the maintenance of ethnic differences in other ways. Allan Knight (1990) argues that early indigenistas, while challenging Eurocentric racism, were not able to break with the categories of European racial science. Although they agreed that Indians and mestizos were not inferior races, they still believed that racial differences were significant. For some indigenistas, Indians and mestizos were superior to whites. Although they challenged Eurocentric hierarchies, they kept a sense of racial difference. Other indigenistas believed in innate differences between the races but refused to assign a hierarchy to these differences. A third position avoided the discussion of racial differences but kept race as a meaningful category. Furthermore, some indigenistas held that all Indians shared a common mental and psychological makeup that was essentially different from that of whites and mestizos.

Two definitions of Indianness were used at the time: a restrictive one that only included groups that retained strong linguistic and cultural characteristics and were often located in "regions of refuge," and a looser one that included peasant groups from central Mexico who were Catholic, bilingual, and greatly influenced by Hispanic culture. According to Knight (1990), although census takers favored the narrower definition, indigenistas preferred the broader one, increasing the numbers of those labeled as Indians. In addition, the romantic valorization of the Indian by Mexican indigenistas and the post-Revolutionary state brought a utilitarian reaction by those labeled as Indians. They were willing to exploit the opportunities offered by official indigenism, even if this meant playing up to romantic official images.

The Mexican state has used the banner of ethnicity to politically mobilize sectors of the peasantry at least since the 1930s (Dawson 1998). The state has promoted organization along ethnic lines in moments of social unrest or weak hegemony (Dietz 1995). After decades of civil war, President Lázaro Cárdenas (1934–1940) used corporatism to consolidate the Revolution. Citizens were incorporated into the state through social organizations (of peasants, workers, urban popular groups, merchants, industrialists, and so forth). Ethnicity was yet another banner under which networks of state clients were created. Cárdenas was the founder of the Councils of Indigenous Peoples, which were affiliated with the ruling party, PRI. The Mexican state lost legitimacy after the 1968 massacre of Tlatelolco Square, when the police killed thousands of protesting radical students and their sympathizers. The next president, Luis Echevarría (1970–1976), launched a radical ethnicist discourse and renewed corporatist practices in an attempt to regain the confidence of the population. Like Cárdenas, he gave new life to PRI-controlled Indigenous Councils. Carlos Salinas de Gortari

(1988–1994) revamped corporatist ethnic organizations in the context of generalized accusations of electoral fraud and regional victories by the political opposition (Dietz 1995).

Another factor that contributed to the reinforcement of ethnic differences was the education of indigenous intellectuals in state institutions to carry out state policies in indigenous regions. The state followed this strategy because earlier community programs implemented by outsiders tended to fail (Hewitt de Alcántara 1984). The unintended consequence of this policy was the formation of a relatively large group of indigenous intellectuals able to lead ethnic movements and articulate ethnic claims.

Classical indigenism had mixed goals and effects. It intended the assimilation of indigenous groups but it perpetuated their separateness from mainstream society. As Gonzalo Aguirre Beltrán notes, "As a matter of fact, indigenism is the result of the conflict and confrontation of contradictory theories. It is neither the forced incorporation of ethnic groups, nor the passive preservation of cultural pluralism that would be accompanied by a policy of reservations and special legislation. . . . On different occasions, indigenism has been accused of being assimilationist or of being culturalist. It is neither one nor the other, but both at the same time" (quoted in Dietz 1995, 38).

The institutional effort of the government officials described in this chapter takes place in the context of the shift toward new indigenism, which started in the 1970s with a renewed focus on the preservation and reinforcement of ethnic identity and social organization. This focus has been present in Mexican indigenism since the 1930s, but it becomes clearly dominant after the 1970s. According to de la Peña (2002), as indigenism shifted ideologically, the Mexican government increased INI's budget and the number of coordinating centers both in the context of a crisis of state legitimacy and in a period of economic boom resulting from skyrocketing oil prices. However, after the 1982 crisis of public finances, worsened by a sharp reduction in oil prices, INI's budget was drastically cut, as were other public services and institutions, in accordance with structural adjustment policies. INI's historical role in regional development waned, and the institution focused on cheaper educational and human rights campaigns, a focus that continues. In the 1990, INI's budget was increased temporarily thanks to funds from the National Solidarity Program, PRONASOL, and the

World Bank. During the Salinas administration (1988–1994), indigenism worked within the framework of the National Solidarity Program. PRONASOL targeted the poorest sectors of the population with development programs intended to reduce the social tensions caused by neoliberal reforms and reinforce the legitimacy of the president (Cornelius, Craig, and Fox 1994). Indians were defined by PRONASOL as the "poorest among the poor," and funds were distributed to them through the National Indigenist Institute (Fox 1994). Meanwhile, constitutional reforms that had contradictory effects on indigenous people were implemented in 1992. The government amended article 27 of the Mexican constitution to end agrarian reform and liberalize the land market, a change that is at the root of the indigenous uprising in Chiapas as well as general discontent in the Mexican countryside (Stephen 2002). Simultaneously, article 4 of the constitution was amended, recognizing for the first time the multicultural character of the Mexican nation and the right of indigenous peoples to preserve their languages, cultures, and forms of social organization. This change is rightly used as evidence by those who interpret new indigenism as a populist discourse intended to distract from unpopular structural reforms. By 1995, INI's budget was drastically reduced again, and the agency was deeply downsized, returning to its focus on training programs (Vázquez León forthcoming). Emiko Saldívar (2002) calls the period that covers the presidencies of Salinas de Gortari and Zedillo (1988–2000) "legal indigenism."

In July 2001 President Vicente Fox approved new legislation on indigenous rights in the context of the negotiations between the Chiapas rebels and the first opposition president since the Revolution. This legislation prohibits ethnic and other forms of discrimination, bases indigenous status on self-identification, gives limited territorial autonomy to indigenous groups, and states the need for affirmative action policies in order to overcome past inequalities. Critics have called this legislation a watered-down version of the San Andrés Accords on Indigenous Rights and Culture, which the government of Ernesto Zedillo signed in 1996 with the Zapatista Army of National Liberation. On May 21, 2003, a decree by President Fox ended the long history of INI and created the Comisión Nacional Para el Desarrollo de los Pueblos Indígenas (CONADEPI) [National Committee for the Development of Indigenous Peoples]. The role of CONADEPI is to advise and coordinate the policies of regular state institutions for indigenous matters. Critics of the presidential decision to close INI argue that, like CONADEPI, INI's original function was to coordinate the work of other state agencies when they addressed indigenous peoples. However, because these agencies neglected indigenous regions, INI progressively assumed their functions (Pérez Ruiz and Argueta Villamar 2003). The foundation of CONADEPI can be interpreted as a continuation of the tendency to reduce INI´s functions to those of advice and coordination, with the corresponding budget cut. Again, the Mexican state demonstrates its populist character by combining progressive legislation that promotes indigenous rights with budget and program cuts in indigenist agencies.

The post-Revolutionary Mexican state is the result of contradictory projects: it originates in a social revolution and bases its legitimacy on the idea that the state is the advocate and benefactor of popular groups, but at the same time it favors businessmen's interests, particularly in the last decades of neoliberal reforms. This tension is reflected at the level of policy, as some government agencies facilitate capitalist development while others carry out advocacy tasks for the downtrodden. However, these projects are not contradictory if one of the tasks of the state in promoting capitalism is to ensure a reasonably healthy and collaborative working class. In the following pages, I focus on those government agencies that advocate for popular groups.

State Institutions in Baja California in the 1990s

The Instituto Nacional Indigenista in Baja California

In Baja California, indigenist institutions are new arrivals; historically, there were few native indigenous people, and they lacked political or economic importance to the state. In the early 1980s, indigenist institutions were brought to the northwest to address the problems of indigenous migrants from the southern states of Oaxaca and Guerrero. At the same time, migrant day laborers and indigenous communities in border cities joined independent labor unions and urban popular movements linked to opposition parties, particularly the left-wing Party of the Democratic Revolution (PRD) (Kearney 1988; Nagengast and Kearney 1990). Significantly, this population became a priority for the federal government in the mid-1980s, when Mexican indigenism began to express an interest in migrant and urban indigenous populations (INI/SEDESOL 1994). This interest turned into law in 2001, with a constitutional amendment that stated the need to protect indigenous migrants, particularly indigenous day laborers. In the 1990s, INI's activities in Baja California included the promotion of the legal rights of migrants, the reinforcement of indigenous civil organizations, programs that improved the situation of indigenous day laborers, and a radio station. It is curious that INI has prioritized serving indigenous day laborers rather than indigenous migrants to cities in Baja California, despite the fact that, according to the 2000 census, there are almost as many indigenous migrants in the city of Tijuana as in the areas of commercial agriculture (Serrano, Embriz, and Fernández 2002). This may be due to the general association of indigenous people with the countryside or to the strategic importance of commercial agriculture to the state and its project of development based on free trade.

THE DIRECTOR.   The office of engineer Suárez, the director of INI in Baja California, is located in the city of Ensenada, not far from the areas of commercial agriculture where indigenous migrants work. Suárez is from a small border town in Baja California. That a northerner was hired for this position in the mid-1990s might have reflected an interest in decentralization on the part of the federal government; this kind of position is often occupied by government officials from the capital city. The quotes that follow are from an interview I conducted with Suárez in August 1997, and from several follow-up conversations.

The engineer presented himself as a practical man and confessed that he was not an intellectual: "In INI we are not doing as much research as we used to do in the past. We are not researching Indian migration or acculturation. We are more interested in addressing the needs and practical problems of indigenous people." In the manner of a scientist, he started to classify indigenous migrants according to the places where they could be found, the economic activities they performed, and whether they were temporary or settled migrants. "You may find them in an urban or rural scenario. In the city they work in construction, domestic service, and street vending. In the countryside they work as day laborers or carry out informal activities. We may also classify them according to whether they are temporary, seasonal, or settled migrants. Temporary migrants may be on their way to the United States, or they may be seasonal workers planning to return to their region of origin." This classification perhaps helped the engineer provide some order to a chaotic situation. Indigenous migrants are a highly mobile population, and the state does not know exactly how many are in Baja California at a given moment. In addition, most indigenous migrants lack birth certificates or any other official documentation. In Baja California, the temporary and settled categories are used by competing state agencies to distribute the indigenous migrant population between them. INI took care of the settled population, whereas PRONSJAG was concerned with temporary workers living in employer provided camps.

Suárez described INI programs in Baja California in the 1990s: "We are investigating human rights abuses against Indians in the migratory route. The police and the army often harass them. We are trying to stop these abuses. We are educating and training migrants to learn their rights and to defend themselves. We want to provide indigenous migrants with a "migrant ID" [cartilla de migrante], so that they are not mistaken for Guatemalan or Salvadoran Indians. Currently, they are not able to demonstrate that they are Mexicans and, therefore, they are victims of constant abuses."

Several aspects of this statement deserve comment. First, Suárez, a government official, presented himself as an advocate for indigenous migrants against other branches of the government, such as the police and the army. Different branches of the government had contradictory purposes: some protected Indians, whereas others harassed them. Interestingly, Suárez did not plan to directly challenge those branches of the government that mistreated indigenous migrants. Instead, he organized migrants to resist government abuses.

Suárez's emphasis on education and training to solve the problems of indigenous peoples reflects budgetary constraints, but it also follows a long tradition within Mexican indigenism. Since the Revolution, indigenistas have emphasized cultural change through formal education as a way to liberate Indians from political and economic oppression. In addition, a focus on education allows the government to support popular groups without directly challenging the power of elites (Hewitt de Alcántara 1984).

The expediting of migrant identification cards was part of a wider government project of registration of the indigenous migrant population that started in the early 1990s (INI-SEDESOL 1994). Registration helped the state know more about this population while it helped migrants claim their citizenship rights. Migrants needed to show official documents to have access to public education, social security, health, and other public services, as well as to be treated as Mexican citizens. Finally, as Suárez noted, registration helped distinguish between Mexican and "foreign" Indians. The former should be treated as citizens. He does not say what would happen to the latter. Would they perhaps face deportation to their countries of origin? As Derek Sayer (1994, 369) has noted, "What comes out most forcefully here is the polysemic, ambiguous, contradictory quality of these putative state forms; even as they oppress, they also empower. It is not a question of either/or but both/and."

Suárez explained that one of the strongest initiatives of INI in the mid-1990s was the Programa de Apoyo a las Organizaciones Civiles [Program in Support of Civil Organizations]. The federal government funded and supported organizations that fought for indigenous rights: "Indians are entitled to the same rights as any other Mexican plus an extra right: the right to difference. INI has programs to reinforce indigenous languages, cultures, and forms of social and political organization. It has radio stations that broadcast in indigenous languages and funds to promote indigenous culture." Then, Suárez confessed that cultural programs had a "secret" objective, to strengthen ethnic identity and social organization: "We would like to consolidate ethnic consciousness and organization. By financing cultural programs, we achieve a greater cohesion within the ethnic groups. Strong social organization helps them fight for their rights. This is not about folklore." Therefore, Suárez understood indigenous culture as an instrument to strengthen the group politically, an understanding that reflects the tradition of radical indigenistas of the 1930s, such as Vicente Lombardo Toledano, who understood ethnicity as a tool for political organization and the liberation of popular groups (Hewitt de Alcántara 1984).

THE ANTHROPOLOGIST. In ways similar to other indigenist government officials, Anselmo, the INI anthropologist in Baja California, did not present himself as a bureaucrat but as a political activist and man of action. He claimed to have been dedicated to political activism from 1985 to 1987, the period during which the union movement flourished in San Quintín and the state made efforts to co-opt it (Millán and Rubio 1992). He explained that he had been forced to leave the region because of his political activities; he returned in 1994 with what he characterized as a more diplomatic and conciliatory approach. The following quotes are from an interview and several follow-up conversations that took place in the summer of 1997.

Anselmo spoke of INI as an institution that genuinely cared for Indians: "There are numerous human rights violations against indigenous day laborers in San Quintín. Indigenous culture is not respected. Sometimes, Indians are jailed because they carry machetes or because they kidnap a woman to marry her, whereas those are common practices in their region of origin. INI defends Indians in these cases and it gets into a lot of trouble for doing it."

He went on to criticize a rival government agency, the National Program in Solidarity with Day Laborers (PRONSJAG) colloquially called Day Laborers', an institution that also addressed the indigenous migrant population in San Quintín. According to Anselmo, Day Laborers' lacked ethnic sensitivity because it was characterized by a class-based approach.[2] Day Laborers', for its part, accused INI of clientelistic and corporatist practices because it used federal funds to encourage the formation of groups of followers faithful to the institution and the PRI. According to de la Rosa (1987), this kind of competition between institutions with similar goals and the same target population has been common in Mexico. Every program and agency aims to co-opt clients, from whom they will then require fidelity and exclusivity. The allocation of public resources is based on the institution's networks and political efficiency; institutions with parallel aims are not interested in joining efforts, which damages the interests of those they serve.

Anselmo explained that the main goal of INI in San Quintín was to promote the education and social organization of indigenous migrants. According to him, the state could not intervene directly in the conflict between agrarian entrepreneurs and day laborers. However, government agencies could educate and secretly organize [grillar] day laborers to resist agrarian capitalism. INI trained indigenous leaders, and a federal program financed the organizations that led the Indian movement in San Quintín. Anselmo continued, "INI has been very independent from the state. There is a rumor, for example, that INI financed the armed uprising in Chiapas.

Probably a lot of that dough [lana] was used to buy weapons." Anselmo's statements illustrate again how the Mexican government works in Baja California. It does not challenge agrarian entrepreneurs directly by forcing them to follow labor laws that protect day laborers and that are ignored most of the time in the valley (Garduño, García, and Morán 1989). However, the federal government promotes social organization to encourage workers to fight for their own rights. In this way, the government does not directly confront the local bourgeoisie, but at the same time it legitimizes itself as the advocate for the downtrodden. All this takes place in the context of national agrarian policies that favor commercial agriculture and exporters with credit and other privileges (Stephen 2002). Moreover, by promoting state-controlled social organization, government institutions incorporate independent political movements that were originally allied to the political opposition. Anselmo explained why INI bases its organizational strategy on ethnicity: "The work of Day Laborers' is limited from the point of view of organization. It creates committees to reach a concrete goal like getting electricity or running water. When the objective is achieved, the organization disappears. INI, on the contrary, works on the basis of ethnicity. If we want to get electricity or running water, the basis of our work is ethnicity. Ethnicity provides more continuity to our actions."

For Anselmo, ethnicity is an effective and lasting banner for state-sponsored social organization because he conceives it as more solid and permanent than other identities, such as class. Paradoxically, he also believes that Indian identity is endangered:

> [Indian] culture is getting lost because it is clandestine. They don't want to be Indians because Indians are fucked up [jodidos]. The day they realize they have a right to their culture, they are going to preserve it. However, we don't pretend to keep them unchanged like museum pieces. They are Baja Californian Mixtecs. It does not matter whether they migrate. They should still preserve their identity. The idea that an ethnic group is tied to its traditional territory is no longer true. Indians do not have territories or sacred places any more, but they are still Indians. Language does not define them either, especially if their language is not functional any more and it is not going to be preserved. We have to privilege consciousness and self-identification.

Anselmo is therefore willing to redefine and expand the category of Indian to maintain ethnic boundaries in a situation of migration and cultural change. Territory (living in a community defined as indigenous) and language in particular are no longer markers of Indianness. Furthermore, indigenous people do not need to stick closely to tradition or culture to remain Indian. The new marker, self-identification, is exactly the one promoted by state agencies. It is also a marker of difference that reinforces boundaries between social groups without focusing on culture content (Barth 1969) and while carefully avoiding a return to the earlier concept of race, which is what ultimately would remain if boundaries were maintained without maintaining cultural differences. Anselmo's understanding of Indian status has been made official by the 2001 constitutional amendments on indigenous rights that choose self-identification as a preferred marker of Indian status in a context in which increasing numbers of indigenous peasants are migrating to work in commercial agriculture (Vázquez León forthcoming).

THE RADIO STATION. The "Voice of the Valley," the INI radio station in San Quintín, is broadcast in Spanish and in the main indigenous languages spoken in the area: Mixtec, Zapotec, Triqui, and Purepecha. The director, Juan, was a young man from Mexico City. The aim of the radio, was to educate indigenous day laborers about their rights. It encouraged them to learn, to organize, and to be proud of their ethnic heritage. The radio, inspired by the principles of new indigenism, had a participatory orientation, and its staff members were indigenous migrants from the different ethnic groups represented in the valley. Moreover, the radio aimed to be an open space for indigenous day laborers. They were welcome to visit its offices, talk on the air about any topics of interest to them, and use a library that specialized in indigenous issues.

Many day laborers in San Quintín spoke highly of the indigenist radio station. Don Eugenio, for example, said, "The radio teaches us about our rights. Thanks to the radio we are becoming civilized Indians who know our rights." He had visited the radio, met its staff, and had been allowed to talk on the air. He explained that day laborers very much enjoyed listening to their portable radios while they were working in the fields. According to Eugenio, the radio was a helpful link between the indigenous communities in Oaxaca, Baja California, and the United States. Through the radio, people were able to find out where relatives were and how they were doing.

An important goal of the federally financed radio station was to redefine and reinforce indigenous identity. Don Eugenio became, in his own words, a "civilized Indian who knows his rights" thanks to the radio. Elderly indigenous migrants with whom I spoke in Baja California still referred to "indigenous people" [*indígenas*] as opposed to "rational people" [*gente de razón*]. An indigenous migrant told me that his wife was *de razón* and *gente civilizada* (a civilized person), meaning that she was mestiza. The colonial terminology that divided the world between gente *de razón* and indígenas was adopted by indigenous people when they learned Spanish, as this example illustrates, and indigenous people also learn other self-derogatory terms as they learn Spanish: For example, indigenous women in Tijuana told me that the Spanish word for "hair" was *greñas*. *Greñas* actually means dirty, uncombed, long hair and it is a word used by Tijuana's middle classes and members of the local police when referring to the hair of these women.

Another form of identity that the radio helps create is that of the "indigenous migrant," also a contradiction from the point of view of traditional understandings of Indianness in post-Revolutionary Mexico, because an Indian who migrated and learned Spanish was expected to become mestizo (Caso 1980). Erasto Rojas (1996), Mixtec producer for the Voice of the Valley, discusses the functions of this institution. He explains that the radio's audience is composed of indigenous migrants who arrive in the north from the poorest states of the nation. Indigenous migrants suffer a double violence: the separation from their communities of origin and the racism of the region of destination. They are treated as foreigners in their own country.[3] The role of the Voice of the Valley, according to Rojas, is to make these experiences of discrimination known. He explained that, as a consequence of racism, indigenous migrants reject their own ethnic identity, "Precisely because [the indigenous person] suffers a constant aggression, he tries to erase the cultural elements that make him different. For example, parents do not teach their children the [Indian] language to spare them the stigmatization that they have suffered." According to Rojas, the objective of the radio is to become a bridge between migrants and their communities of origin so that they would be partially spared the suffering of separation. Thus, the radio aims to reinforce the transnational community by keeping migrants in Baja California and in the United States in touch with those who stay behind in Oaxaca and Guerrero. A second objective is to teach indigenous people that it is fine to be Indian, that they should not be ashamed of their ethnic identity: "The radio must be a space where [indigenous] people speak their language. If we accept that culture is constantly transformed and recreated, then the radio contributes to the construction of a new cultural identity: that of the 'indigenous migrant'" (Rojas 1996, 121).

According to Juan , however, the radio he directs also needs to adapt to the acculturation process that indigenous migrants are going through, or it would risk losing its audience. Migrant Indians, according to Juan, prefer northern Mexican music to music from Oaxaca. Juan adds that Oaxacan migrants perceive everything northern as a symbol of modernity and status. Judging from a number of programs that I had listened to, the radio does not have an essentialist understanding of ethnicity. For example, it encourages indigenous women to get educated and struggle against domestic violence and sexism, even if this means a transformation of their traditional way of life, as illustrated by this excerpt from a Voice of the Valley broadcast (August 1997):

> Perhaps he does not know that a woman is equal to a man. That she has the same rights and opportunities. That she deserves respect. Besides, International Labor Organization Convention 169 and the Constitution state that women and men have the same rights. This is what I tell Doña Rosa, but she says: "What can we do? This is the custom that we indigenous people have always had." "Yes, it is important to respect our traditions, when they are good, but we have to start to understand that you, women, also have the right to take decisions."

An additional function of the radio is to connect the indigenous migrant population with the state and to mediate between social groups. Juan told us that the radio was originally used by the state to get in touch with isolated populations that could not be reached by other means. In San Quintín, it is an effective tool to publicize government programs and institutions. Juan explains that the radio has an important political function: to mediate between social groups in conflict. It is most often used by day laborers to denounce the daily abuses of agrarian entrepreneurs. Entrepreneurs, according to Juan, keep their distance from the radio. However, Juan assured me, entrepreneurs had supported the radio on occasion and were welcome to participate. "The radio makes possible a conversation between workers and employers," he said. Despite these diplomatic intentions, the radio is generally perceived as an advocate, and a quite radical one, of day laborers. When I was conducting fieldwork in San Quintín, the radio stopped working properly because of technical problems. There was a rumor among day laborers that entrepreneurs had sabotaged it. Even engineer Suárez, the director of INI in Baja California, said that these rumors might be well founded. Some programs were actually quite radical: they started with the revolutionary anthem, "The International," and then encouraged agrarian workers to strike against agro-export entrepreneurs, a remarkable statement to be made by a state institution!

The General Directorate of Indigenous Education of the Department of Public Education

While doing fieldwork in a neighborhood in the city of Tijuana inhabited by indigenous and mestizo migrants, I noticed that the indigenous public school was the most influential state institution for indigenous migrants. The principal and the teachers were Mixtecs from Oaxaca and leaders in Tijuana's indigenous movement.

Since the 1920s, the Department of Public Education (SEP) has been in close contact with indigenous populations. The post-Revolutionary state aimed to make public education universal in order to produce proud Mexican citizens ready to participate in a modern economy that required literacy skills. Because of a belief that the problems of poor indigenous populations could be solved primarily through education, SEP became one of the first representatives of the state in rural indigenous areas (Hewitt de Alcántara 1984). However, as Lynn Stephen (2002) has shown, the public school system was unevenly instituted in different regions. It is often argued that the public school system promoted the cultural assimilation of indigenous populations (e.g., Bonfil Batalla 1990; Díaz Polanco 1997; Hernández Castillo 2001). Judith Friedlander (1975) has argued that public schools had a mixed impact on indigenous identity. According to Friedlander, schools taught Spanish and Western values to Nahuatl-speaking peasants, while marking them as different through school festivals presented for outside authorities, where they were encouraged to dress as Indians and perform Indian dances. In addition, teachers produced knowledge that conveyed sharp ethnic differences to urban mestizo audiences. Since the 1970s, the General Directorate of Indigenous Education (DGEI), a section of SEP, has claimed to be interested in the preservation of indigenous languages, cultures, and forms of social and political organization, following the spirit of new indigenism (SEP-DGEI 1996). In 1992, article 4 of the Mexican constitution was reformed, acknowledging that Mexico was a multicultural nation. Public education tried to measure up to this statement. SEP perceived the ethnic and national projects as complementary. According to SEP publications (SEP-DGEI 1996), public education should "balance the ethnic and national dimensions." It should teach students love for their nation and appreciation for national history, symbols, and institutions while reinforcing and protecting Indian languages and cultures.

Despite SEP's multicultural and proethnic discourse, indigenous education has been plagued by contradictions. For example, a pamphlet advertising indigenous education contained illustrations of archeological remains, symbolically placing indigenous peoples in a remote past. None of the pictures in the pamphlet portrayed contemporary indigenous groups. SEP asserted that indigenous languages should be used exclusively during the first three years of elementary school and be combined with Spanish in subsequent years. This statement did not translate into daily practices in indigenous public schools in Baja California. In the school where I worked, Spanish was the only language used for teaching after kindergarten. Indigenous languages were used occasionally either to communicate with monolingual parents or to exchange a few words with a child who was still monolingual. In fact, SEP documents acknowledge that there are many obstacles for the implementation of bilingual education. First, educators must come to terms with a legacy of assimilation policies and practices. Second, according to SEP, most indigenous parents wish their children to assimilate and speak only Spanish. Third, a number of indigenous languages are not standardized but are fragmented into dialects— sometimes a dialect for each community—that are not mutually understandable. Finally, in Baja California, indigenous children from several ethnic groups share the same classroom. Often, children do not belong to the same ethnic group or do not speak the same dialect as their teachers. Indigenous teachers may protect indigenous children from discrimination by mestizo educators, but they do not secure bilingual education for them.

THE DIRECTOR OF DGEI.   The following quotes are from an interview I conducted in the summer of 1997. Licenciado Rodríguez, director of the DGEI in Baja California, started the interview by explaining that he owed his job to his political skills: he had successfully negotiated a conflict between mestizo, migrant indigenous, and native Baja Californian teachers. Migrant indigenous teachers argued that only Indians should teach indigenous children and that they were the only ones prepared to teach in indigenous languages. Rodríguez acknowledged that most education took place in Spanish anyway. He believed that migrant indigenous teachers were struggling for their jobs more than for indigenous languages or cultures. Despite his cynicism, Rodríguez, following neo-indigenist SEP guidelines, believed that indigenous cultures and languages should be preserved. However, he did not believe that indigenous culture was something that indigenous people possessed and that the school system should pick up from them, cherish, and reproduce. On the contrary, he argued that public schools needed to teach indigenous culture to the grassroots: "We want the teacher to merge into the community and assume its leadership. We want to train community leaders. We need to take their traditional culture to the community and teach them Indian culture." This also illustrates how SEP, like INI, linked the promotion of indigenous culture with state-sponsored political organization. This approach worked well in Baja California because the Mixtec teachers brought by SEP from Oaxaca in 1982 have been the organizers and leaders of the state's indigenous movement.

I asked Rodríguez what he understood by "indigenous culture." He spoke first about tequio (communal work obligations). He said, "Indians do not like modern individualism. They feel that they have the right and the duty to share with others. They are governed by the principles of generosity and the common good." Rodríguez's discourse resonates with the importance that the Mexican government gives to tequio in its definition of Indian culture. Interestingly, according to Collier (1994), the concept of unpaid communal work has been used by the state to extract labor from indigenous communities for public works from the colonial period to the present. In the same way, in the neighborhood were I did fieldwork, fathers of schoolchildren worked in the construction of the public school in their spare time. If somebody was unable to fulfill his duty, he was expected to pay somebody else to work for him. Mothers and grandmothers worked in school maintenance and in the organization of school life. Communal work and community participation often meant that unpaid labor was extracted from the community, but the state took credit for providing school infrastructure and maintenance. Unpaid communal work was also expected from poor mestizos. However, when addressing an indigenous population, the rhetoric of tequio was deployed to encourage people to participate.

Rodríguez had a folkloric and romantic understanding of ethnicity. He said enthusiastically that he loved Indian celebrations because everybody participated in them and they were beautiful and colorful. These "Indian" celebrations were enacted periodically in every public school. Folkloric holidays were used to promote nationalism through the celebration of ethnic difference. Indigenous dances from different states of the Republic were selected and performed forming a colorful Mexican pastiche. As SEP pamphlets have done, Rodríguez placed indigenous cultures in the past. He compared indigenous languages to Latin and Greek, which "are still important even though they are dead." He claimed, nevertheless, that Indians should not be kept frozen in the past. The role of the public school was to introduce Indians to modernity. Like INI officials, Rodríguez claimed that indigenous languages should not be what marks a person as an Indian, "Even if a child does not speak an Indian language, he is still an Indian. Indigenous education should take care of him. It is not fair that Indians jump to mestizo and then to Indian again [*no se vale que estén saltando de indio a mestizo y luego a indio de nuevo*]." If Indians do not speak a different language, why should they need special education? What makes them different in Rodríguez's eyes? Is it their culture (communal solidarity, celebrations, and so on) or their physical makeup?

THE INDIAN SCHOOL. The principal and teachers of Valle Verde's indigenous public school were Mixtecs from the state of Oaxaca. They arrived in Tijuana in 1982 when they were hired by SEP to serve the indigenous migrant community. SEP wished Mixtec educators to teach Spanish and help

Mixtec migrants assimilate to Tijuana's urban society. Nevertheless, indigenous teachers have been instrumental in the reproduction of ethnic boundaries in Baja California. Since 1984, they have been the leaders and organizers of Tijuana's indigenous movement (Kearney 1988; Nagengast and Kearney 1990; Velasco 2002). In addition, to demonstrate the need for new indigenous schools in the city, they have marked the migrant community as Indian when they have taken population censuses.

As an example of the organizational history of these teachers, I will summarize the background of Julio, the school's principal. He was born in a small community in the Mixteca region and was trained by INI in a boarding school as an indigenous *promotor* (community organizer and developer). He worked for INI for a few years and was later hired by SEP as a bilingual teacher. He joined several PRI-affiliated organizations like the Movimiento Juvenil Revolucionario [Juvenile Revolutionary Movement] and the Confederación Nacional Campesina (CNC) [National Peasant Confederation]. When he arrived in Tijuana, he founded the (Asociación de Mixtecos Residentes en Tijuana (ASMIRT) [Association of Mixtecs Living in Tijuana] with other Mixtec teachers and a mestizo anthropologist and, later, a Comité Comunitario de Planeación (COCOPLA) [Community Planning Committee]. ASMIRT was a relatively independent popular urban movement sympathetic to the PRD, whereas COCOPLA was created after President Miguel de la Madrid (1982–1988) encouraged indigenous people to organize such committees in order to put participatory indigenism into effect. Later, the principal collaborated with PAN through a neighborhood organization, and he was fond of the work of this party at the local level. The principal did not perceive his collaboration with rival political parties as a problem. On the contrary, he claimed that the poor cannot afford to be faithful to a single party because they should look for benefits from different politicians.

The history of the creation of Valle Verde's school shows that indigenous education is not treated like regular education in Baja California. An article in the journal *Comunidad Educativa* explains how Julio founded the school (Montiel Aguirre 1995): First he went to the neighborhood to take a census of the indigenous population to show SEP that there was need for an indigenous school. Then he organized indigenous parents in a committee to pressure the authorities. Julio and the committee of parents visited several state institutions to ask for support for their project. PRODUTSA (Promotora de Desarrollo Urbano de Tijuana S.A., Tijuana's Urban Development Corporation) donated the lot on which the school was to be built. SEP donated construction materials, Tijuana's city hall donated $800, INI donated $250, and a nongovernmental organization donated $325. Teachers and parents contributed their labor to the construction of the school. The classrooms were made of cheap construction materials, and the school still lacked bathrooms, running water, drainage, and furniture. Then Julio and the committee of parents went to regular schools to ask for old furniture. SEP gave them some old chairs. Authorities from different state institutions, however, presided over the inauguration ceremony of Valle Verde's school and took credit for its construction.

Several aspects of Julio's account deserve comment. First, Indians do not seem to receive public education as a citizenship right. They have to visit offices and institutions to ask for favors to have access to their constitutional right to education. These favors leave the community indebted to particular authorities. Indian education also seems to be a form of charity: Indians were given old furniture to equip their school. Community participation meant that indigenous people had to volunteer and provide for themselves what the state had the responsibility to provide for them. Nevertheless, once the school was constructed, it joined the statistics of what the state had done for indigenous people.

The philosophy of the school was contradictory. Julio explained in an interview (September 1996) that he aimed to strengthen indigenous languages and cultures in Valle Verde. When I first arrived in the neighborhood, Julio showed me beautifully illustrated textbooks that he was planning to use in his classes. They were edited by SEP and written in a dialect of the Mixtec language spoken in the mountains of Guerrero, the region from which most of the children in the neighborhood came. Later, I realized that these luxury editions were never used in the classroom. Valle Verde's teachers spoke a different dialect of the Mixtec language and were unable to use the books. Those children who did speak the dialect in which the books were written did not know how to read or write in it. The books were used exclusively to show visitors (like me) that indigenous language and culture were taught at the school. In an article published by Arthur Golden (1996) in the *San Diego Union Tribune*, Julio presented himself as a leader who fought for the preservation of the Mixtec language. Golden compared bilingual education in the United States and Baja California. He argued that, in the United States, bilingual education was used to assimilate children into the English-language mainstream. In Baja, in contrast, it meant teaching children in native languages to secure their linguistic survival. Despite good intentions, all classes in Julio's school were taught in Spanish. Daily communication between teachers, children, and parents took place in Spanish unless somebody was unable to understand it. The only exception was a workshop in which Julio taught children the Mixtec alphabet, the Mexican national anthem translated into the Mixtec language, and some scattered words in Mixtec. This workshop was originally scheduled twice a week, but it took place only a few times while I was in Tijuana. Julio acknowledged that parents were not enthusiastic about his project. He wrote, "Last year, many parents did not like the fact that their children were taught the Mixtec language in school. They argued that their language was not good and they showed contempt for their own culture. The loss of these values is due to lack of consciousness and the influence of North American culture" (Julio, Project of Mixtec Language Workshop written for SEP). Julio added that indigenous migrants should be encouraged to remain indigenous even against their own will. The preservation of native languages became a nationalist project as Julio warned about the danger of their being replaced by North American cultural elements.

As in an earlier period described by Friedlander (1975), Indian identity surfaced in Valle Verde's school during festivals and celebrations, when children were encouraged to dress as Indians and to dance for outsiders, especially local politicians and government officials. Valle Verde's children, however, were not dressed as Mixtecs (their own ethnic group) but as Aztecs or Yaquis. They were encouraged to assume a generic Indian identity that had little relationship to their specific experiences or traditions. This generic Indian identity was part of a larger repertoire of Mexican national symbols, illustrating another instance in which the ethnic and the national complemented each other.

Julio asked me to collaborate with him in a cultural recovery workshop that he was planning to carry out in Valle Verde. Our work was to gather and record the experiences and traditions of Mixtec elderly and children. He wrote a proposal for SEP stating that he had a commitment to recover and publicize the culture of his forefathers. He wished to raise consciousness in Mexican society about the existence of native peoples while convincing Mixtec children of the importance of their own culture so they would no longer be ashamed of being Indians. However, the topics that he proposed for discussion in the workshop had little relationship to the specific experiences of Mixtec children or the elderly in Valle Verde. They were "The Day of the Dead," "The Mexican Revolution," "Christmas," "The National Symbols" (the flag and the anthem), "The Life of President Benito Juárez," "The Panamerican Day of the Indian," "Labor Day," "Mother's Day," "Women as the Basis of the Family," "The Education of Indians," and the "Day of the Teacher." Most of these were themes celebrated in public schools throughout Mexico and not issues specific to the Mixtec ethnic group. Some had an indigenous flavor, but they were part of a generic representation of the Indian for national consumption.

Julio started his cultural recovery workshop by explaining the meaning of being Mexican to indigenous children. He continued by arguing that Indians had the right to be treated as real Mexicans. Then he referred to the reform of Mexican constitution's article 4, which defines Mexico as a multicultural nation:

> In Mexico, there are many cultures and languages, but only one official language that is Spanish. With this language you can communicate with all Mexican children. But you should also remember that each culture has its own language. We should learn to respect them. We want them to respect us. We want them not to laugh at those of us who do not speak Spanish well. We should be conscious that the nation is multicultural and that we should respect the children who speak poor Spanish or who do not read well. The compromise is that they should learn, they should improve themselves everyday. (Julio, fieldwork notes taken by the author during Cultural Recovery Workshop, November 1996)

Like other government officials, Julio combined the ethnic and the national project. His aim was to integrate Indians into the Mexican nation as citizens. As Friedlander (1975) argued for Nahuatl speakers in Morelos, Julio understood indigenous culture as a "lack," for example, a lack of proficiency and reading ability in Spanish, rather than something positive that indigenous people had. Interestingly, in the preceding quote, Julio identifies himself and his audience first with mestizos who should respect Indians, later with indigenous people who demand respect, and finally with mestizos again, reflecting the contradictions and complexities of his discourse as well as the perceived need for children to identify simultaneously with mestizo Mexico and disadvantaged indigenous people.

Julio's understanding of indigenous culture, as well as the understanding of other Mixtec teachers with whom I had the opportunity to interact, emphasized boundaries between indigenous and mestizo more than culture content (proficiency in the Mixtec language was not sought, children were marked as Indians while embodying the symbols of other ethnic groups, indigenous teachers were not able to explain to me what the actual components of indigenous culture were, nationalist symbols replaced Mixtec traditions and experiences, and so on). This fact resonates with Fredrik Barth's (1969) classic analysis of ethnicity, applied by Friedlander (1975) to the case of indigenous Mexicans; this analysis holds that boundaries between groups, and not culture content, are the politically significant factor. This hollowed-out ethnicity is not threatening to the nationalist project of the state but instead complements it.

The Department of Popular Cultures

Anthropologist Eugenia had a reputation for knowing the popular groups in Baja California well. She started as an employee of the Department of Popular Cultures and soon became its director for the north of Mexico. I took notes on her approach to indigenous issues on two occasions. The first was a presentation she made at a conference in the fall of 1996. The second was an in-depth interview that I recorded in January 1997.

The Department of Popular Cultures (colloquially called Culturas Populares) was founded in 1977 by critical anthropologists Guillermo Bonfil Batalla and Rodolfo Stavenhagen according to the principles of participatory indigenism. Its main goal is to promote the cultures, languages, and arts of indigenous peoples. That the word "popular" was chosen to mean mainly "Indian" points to the close association between ethnicity and class in contemporary Mexico. Culturas Populares works in two directions. It sponsors and publishes research on indigenous cultures with the aim of strengthening the plural character of Mexican national identity. In

addition, the institution stimulates ethno-development. It trains indigenous leaders to organize cultural centers, workshops, meetings, language
classes, and other cultural events that it funds (Dietz 1995).

Eugenia associated ethnicity with social class. She argued, for example,
that a middle-class Indian could not exist in Mexico and emphasized that
Mexican Indians are extremely poor and uneducated. She understood Indians with property as deviants. Indians with education were expected to
integrate automatically with mestizo Mexico. She said, "If an Indian is rich,
it is because he steals the goods of the community. If an Indian receives an
education, he is no longer an Indian. He becomes integrated to national
society. Indians are harassed and discriminated both as Indians and as
poor people. They are often perceived as poor people who endure harsh
living conditions and as a cheap labor force." Therefore, according to
Eugenia, poverty and lack of formal education were necessary conditions
for an individual to be defined as Indian. Her ideas should be placed in the
context of widespread anthropological assumptions that Indians reject
capital accumulation and that their societies are essentially egalitarian
(e.g., Bonfil Batalla 1990; Varese 1996). An Indian who accumulates wealth
is expected to reinvest the surplus in the community through solidarity
practices and ceremonial consumption. The idea that Indians do not wish
to accumulate wealth is problematic; it does not reflect the reality of indigenous people, the majority of whom wish to improve economically and are
business-oriented. Indians are constructed as utopian moral beings and
not as regular individuals. Furthermore, the belief that Indians are frugal
may help justify their poverty or the fact that they are offered low salaries.

Eugenia affirmed, in front of a Mixtec school principal who was an important leader in the indigenous movement in Baja California and whom
she knew well because they often collaborated in cultural events, that an
educated Indian is no longer Indian. Did Eugenia think that the Mixtec
leader was not a real Indian anymore? Or did she think that he was not
really educated? According to Eugenia, indigenous culture needed to be
pure and bounded. She perceived exposure to Western culture via formal
education as a threat to this cultural heritage.

Eugenia understood Indians as different, vulnerable individuals who
should be segregated in order to be protected from racist attacks and dangerous outside influences that threatened the purity of their culture. She

believed that integration was neither possible (mestizos would not allow Indians to integrate as equals) nor desirable (Indians would lose their authenticity). It is interesting that in her remarks Eugenia did not propose to punish people for making racist attacks against Indians in order to allow them to integrate. She stated,

> Racism leads them [Indians] to take refuge in their own spaces, to preserve their languages and identities intact. . . . We should recognize that they are a different culture, that their way of thinking, their interests, are different. When they contact people who think differently from them, this outside people completely destroy their worldview [*cosmovisión*]. We are, thus, limiting them. When Indians attempt to integrate, they lose what is theirs, and they do not acquire what is ours. They lose their traditional medicine and do not have access to medical attention. They lose their language and they do not speak Spanish well. They are illiterate. They lose what is theirs and they do not acquire anything in return.

These comments suggest that Eugenia did not support the creation of legislation that would guarantee Indians access to health care or formal education so that they would gain access to "what is ours." Her solution was to keep them separate from mestizo society and to preserve their ancestral practices. This meant that Indians would be excluded from mainstream services, opportunities, and resources.

I asked her directly whether she would favor laws and public policies that would guarantee access to formal education and jobs for indigenous people. She answered, "That's a United States thing. There are other processes going on there. North American Indians have had access to education and are more integrated to mainstream culture than indigenous people in Mexico. Here, the Indian worldview is still very different from that of the Mexican. We are talking about totally different cultures." Thus, her understanding that Indians and non-Indians are essentially different led her to accept the exclusion of Indians from the educational system and mainstream jobs. Interestingly, she recognized that native North Americans had been integrated into larger national processes, whereas she implied that Mexican Indians who were Catholic, bilingual migrants, had not.

Eugenia insisted that Indians should be protected from dangerous out-side influences. "Outside people, like religious sects or private develop-ment projects, divide the community. There are rules in the indigenous community that preclude outsiders from having access to public appoint-ments or to the land. However, mestizos have infiltrated the community. Some of them manipulate Indians politically. They are people who have political contacts, people who have support from certain leaders who want to become candidates." This implies that Indians are perceived as passive, naive persons who can be easily manipulated by outsiders. Eugenia understood them not as individuals who were free to associate with anyone they wanted but as childlike beings who needed to be protected from bad influences.

Although Eugenia argued that Indians wanted to be by themselves, she also acknowledged that migrant and urban Indians wished to become mes-tizo to escape racism, "They do not transmit their language. They are iden-tified by their language. They want other things. They want to learn English. They want to become educated and to be able to work in factories. Although some are political and want to keep their culture, most are losing it. Even bilingual teachers do not teach the [indigenous] language to their children." Contradicting her earlier statements, Eugenia acknowledged here that indigenous peoples would like to study and find good jobs and that they perceive their ethnicity as an obstacle to social mobility.

In spite of this, Eugenia believed that indigenous cultures should be preserved because of their value to the Mexican nation: "We have to pre-vent the loss of the culture of our country. If we lose indigenous cultures, it is not only Indians who lose. The world loses." Her comments suggest that indigenous people should not be allowed to make their own decisions about whether to keep their culture or to integrate and that this decision should be made by state institutions for them.

Despite Eugenia's commitment to the principles of new indigenism, she lacked confidence in the abilities and judgment of Indians, "They lack organization and reflection. As a consequence of their history of oppres-sion, some are aggressive and do not want to collaborate with the institu-tions. They are divided in their struggle for power and fight among themselves instead of confronting the problems that affect them. Further-more, the majority of them are not interested in the preservation of their languages and cultures. The media influences them and, in many communities, they do not want to speak the [indigenous] language."

Although Eugenia was the director of an important official institution, she criticized the government because it was unable or unwilling to improve the living and working conditions of Indians, it repressed indigenous movements, and it harassed indigenous individuals. The government, she noted, politically manipulated ethnic groups, "Indians are tired because they are only taken into account in election periods. They are tired of promises and lack of results. We, the institutions, lose our credibility if we do not deliver." Eugenia presented herself as an advocate for the Indians against the government. However, she also thought that the government (the good parts of it) was the only agent that should deal with indigenous people. The rest were outside people who corrupted and threatened the community.

Eugenia described the programs of the Department of Popular Cultures. The institution offered workshops on indigenous languages and literatures and on the recovery of Indian history. Culturas Populares granted scholarships to indigenous individuals to attend these workshops. In addition, Culturas Populares supported traditional holidays, performances, and ceremonies. In the early 1980s, Culturas Populares started to promote the celebration of the Day of the Dead in the oldest indigenous migrant neighborhood in Tijuana, Colonia Obrera. Today, this holiday is considered a grassroots celebration and a sign of the strength of migrant Indian identity. The department promotes indigenous crafts and community museums and sponsors exhibits for the mainstream public. Through distribution of such resources as scholarships and funding for cultural projects, the Department of Popular Cultures is able to contribute to the reinforcement of indigenous identity.

While I was doing fieldwork, I observed that the department was very concerned with public relations. It produced fancy flyers and posters to advertise its programs. In fact, the majority of its staff was expert in communications and design. On occasion, the department posted beautiful posters to announce activities that did not take place. Did Culturas Populares produce propaganda to prove that the government was doing things for indigenous people, especially after the Chiapas uprising?

To sum up, Eugenia was interested in the preservation of ethnic boundaries even in the face of what she believed were the desires of indigenous people. She understood ethnic identity as essentially different, bounded, and endangered, and she perceived poverty and lack of formal education as preconditions for ethnic status. She supported the reproduction of differences for two reasons: first, Indian cultures did not belong to Indians but to the nation, and the preservation of Indian cultures strengthened the national good and the national project of state formation; second, the preservation of ethnic boundaries protected Indians from racism. Protection through segregation also meant exclusion from resources and opportunities, however. The Department of Popular Cultures contributes to the construction and diffusion of state-sanctioned forms of ethnic identity through education, community organizing, and consciousness raising. Economic resources are distributed to gratify those who assume the forms of identity promoted by the government. In addition, the propaganda produced by Popular Cultures is intended to prove that the Mexican government is working for indigenous migrants. This is a case in which the construction of difference and the segregation of those marked as different, allegedly against their own wishes, implies both hierarchy and exclusion from social resources. This idea of protection through segregation and not through fair integration has colonial roots in the *Repúblicas de Indios* created by the Spanish Crown to protect indigenous populations but also to mark them as different and subordinate.

Conclusion

I have shown that some government officials—including indigenous leaders working for the state or collaborating closely with it—in Baja California are interested in, and working for, the reproduction of ethnic boundaries. However, there seem to be two different indigenisms at work. Mestizo government officials easily identify with the government, although this is not without contradictions as they also claim to be working against the government. Indigenous brokers do not tend to present themselves as part of the government, but rather as spokespeople for the indigenous community. Perhaps, as Emiko Saldívar (2002) has noted, indigenista work automatically suggests an unspoken mestizo identity, which makes it difficult for indigenous government officials to assume an indigenista personality.

Whereas some but not all mestizo government officials are parternalistic and hold a static and stereotypical view of Indianness that implies enduring exclusion from regular citizenship rights, indigenous leaders working for the state seem to have a more fluid understanding of their own and their community's distinctiveness, although they are not free from the fear of stigmatization and the wish to belong to the nation as equals through the path of integration. On occasion, they too encourage children to perform mainstream stereotypes and help reinforce differences that in the context of Baja California are easily translated into social hierarchies. State-sponsored ethnicity is often understood as a grassroots product because the voice of the teachers and other leaders trained by the state is taken as a grassroots point of view. That these leaders work for the government and promote government agendas is not sufficiently acknowledged in the literature; nor is their complex intermediate position.

I argue that those who articulate identity more aggressively are principally those who have a vested interest in bureaucratic positions that require or reward the articulation of indigenous identity; in ways similar to the Native Alaskans studied by Dombrowski (2001), those who pay a price for their ethnic identification are more likely to be "against culture," or, in other words, they are likely to be against being identified with a particular culture. Many indigenous migrants would like to assimilate into the mainstream in the north of Mexico in order to move up the socioeconomic ladder or, perhaps, to connect themselves to the modern as they perceive it. This differs from findings in some influential literature on indigenous peoples and the state in Latin America: according to a number of authors, indigenous communities resist the state's efforts to assimilate them. In these cases the reinforcement of ethnicity is interpreted as a liberating project (see, for example, Díaz Polanco 1997; Stavenhagen 1994; Stephen 2002; Urban and Sherzer 1992; Van Cott 1994, 2000). In Baja California, some government agencies strengthen ethnic boundaries in a political-economic context in which the indigenous label implies marginalization in rural and urban labor markets.

Baja Californian government officials perceive the national and ethnic projects as complementary rather than contradictory. For example, INI and SEP use ethnicity to sponsor more durable forms of state-controlled social and political organization. Indigenous teachers recover indigenous cultures by teaching about the Mexican constitution, the flag, Benito Juárez, and the national anthem, which they translate into the Mixtec language. Culturas Populares holds that the preservation of the ethnic, even against the will of those so labeled, is central to the national project.

As conceived by some government officials in Baja California, ethnicity is neither a way to recognize the other nor a space for the other's voice. A generic and stereotypical identity is often imposed on migrant communities. It is an empty understanding of ethnicity that focuses more on boundaries between groups than on culture content (Barth 1969; Friedlander 1975). SEP aims to teach indigenous culture to the grassroots instead of learning it from them. INI officials in Baja California have a more fluid understanding of "Indianness," one in which some elements are preserved or reinvented whereas others are transformed. This selective understanding, in which positive traits are encouraged and negative traits are discarded, is also a tradition coming from classical indigenism. The work of state institutions is diverse, and I think this diversity originates in the political position of particular bureaucrats as well as in the history and tradition of particular state institutions. Thus, it is important not to generalize, although there does seem to be a common national project: the reinforcement of ethnic differences. However, the meaning of these differences and what they imply from a socioeconomic point of view could differ depending on the political agendas of individual bureaucrats and institutions.

The government officials who participated in this study feared that ethnic boundaries might dissolve with migration to the border region. They were willing to redefine and expand the category of "Indian" to keep migrants indigenous. For post-Revolutionary indigenism, an "Indian" is a person closely affiliated with a community defined as indigenous who speaks a native language. A migrant who learns Spanish automatically becomes a mestizo. Some Baja Californian government officials redefine Indian status as a matter of consciousness and social organization and de-emphasize the importance of language and territory. Others just claim that an Indian is an Indian and will continue to be so, regardless of cultural transformations. This latter interpretation may suggest an unintended return to the earlier concept of race.

The official redefinition of what it means to be Indian in order to make this label more inclusive contrasts with Stephen's (1997) study of Chiapas in the same time period. According to her, during the 1990s the Mexican state made its definition of Indian less inclusive in order to avoid exceptions to the process of privatization of communal land, a process from which communities defined as indigenous were excluded, as well as to contain the indigenous movement.[4] Perhaps, as Knight (1990) has noted, the state has been working with two definitions of Indian status, one more restrictive than the other, and one or the other has been used strategically depending on the circumstances. For instance, Hernández Castillo (2001) argues that a broader definition of Indianness—one that does not take into account whether people speak a native language or wear an Indian outfit—is used by government officials in the southern Chiapas border region, where indigenous languages and dress have been lost as a result of earlier aggressive assimilation practices. Like Baja California, this is an area where Indians work as peons for meager wages. In a later work, Stephen (2002, 87) notes that the Mexican state still uses objective criteria—particularly language, but also territory, dress, and custom—to identify a person as indigenous.

> Concepts of ethnicity used by the Mexican government continue to rely on trait recognition and the certification by experts of indigenous legitimacy. Obviously this method is about forty years behind anthropological concepts of ethnicity, which focus on the expression and practice of ethnic identity in action and on the process of identity construction. . . . Language is still a significant, but not necessarily the primary ingredient of ethnic identity in eastern Chiapas, particularly in areas where indigenous and peasant organizing has grown over the past twenty years. Second and third generation Tojolabales may not speak Tojolabal, yet they have a strong sense of ethnic identity.

In contrast to Stephen's findings for the south of Mexico, some government officials in Baja California share what Stephen characterizes as current anthropological understandings of ethnic identity. They rely less on language, territory, and other visible traits and more on self-identification, consciousness, and social organization, factors that a number of government agencies are reinforcing. It is interesting that President Fox, who as an agrarian producer has a vested interest in commercial agriculture and the figure of the indigenous day laborer, has transformed this broader understanding of Indian status into constitutional law. It is important also to note here the great capacity of Mexican state institutions to learn from their critics, if not to co-opt them.

Corrigan and Sayer (1985, 3) argue that "states" are able to state: "The arcane rituals of a court of law, the formulae of royal assent to an Act of Parliament, visits of school inspectors, are all statements. They define in great detail acceptable forms and images of social activity and individual and collective identity; they regulate . . . much . . . of social life. In this sense "the State" never stops talking." William Roseberry (1994, 364) warns that Corrigan and Sayer's discussion of the state may not apply to Latin America: "[T]he forms of regulation and routine to which Corrigan and Sayer allude depend on an extremely dense, centralized and effective state. This too has been rare in Mexico, despite the intentions, projects, and claims of the state and its officials in various periods." Similarly, Striffler (2002) shows that the Ecuadorian state was not able to give shape to durable identities in the twentieth century because it was too weak to cover all national territory, and the actions of different branches of government were incoherent and often contradictory. However, this chapter demonstrates that Baja Californian state institutions and government officials are quite efficient in shaping identities and forms of social and political organization based on these identities. They encourage the adoption of certain forms of ethnic identity through the distribution of jobs and resources to leaders and the grassroots. INI finances ethnic civil organizations. SEP provides jobs for indigenous teachers who work on the reinforcement of ethnicity. The media, publications, and public performances also promote ethnic identities; for example, the indigenist radio station plays a key role in the construction of new indigenous identities and in the reinforcement of transnational and transregional identities at the Mexican border.

This evidence also calls into question the thesis of the weakening of the state in the context of globalization. As Aretxaga (2003) has argued, the state has kept its power and allure despite the intensification of transnational interactions and even when its functions have been reduced and privatized. Aretxaga highlights the repressive power of the state in recent decades and the resilient power of the concept of the state as an object of desire. I argue that in the context of globalization the state is not only repressive but also creative: the institutions of the Mexican state are able to shape identities, such as that of the indigenous day laborer or the indigenous migrant, that adapt well to novel global political-economic contexts, such as the national emphasis on commercial agriculture for export. Thus, I suggest that there is a connection between the efforts of several state institutions in Baja California to reinforce an indigenous identity in a context of migration and cultural change and the interests of local and global capitalists who consciously seek an indigenous labor force for certain jobs. However, this connection is complex and ambivalent: it is also a fact that the state unionizes day laborers and empowers them to resist rural capitalism, be able to claim their citizenship rights, and fashion new identities that are able to heal colonial wounds. As Sayer (1994, 376) notes, "[S]tate forms or enactments do not merely constrain. They may also empower and enable. . . . Individuals and groups may creatively adapt and use the forms through which, on another level, they are confined and constrained."

The work of state institutions in Baja California can also be interpreted from another point of view. Alan Knight (1998) has characterized Mexican populism as a political style, a variable mixture between pro-people rhetoric and more or less limited redistribution practices. The discourses and practices of government officials in Baja California illustrate one of the ways in which the populist state works. Different state institutions carry out what seem to be contradictory tasks. Some repress indigenous migrants, whereas others defend them. According to officials who act as advocates for indigenous migrants, repressive agencies of the state have more power and resources than do activist branches, particularly after the 1995 budget crisis (de la Peña 2002). In addition, activist branches of the state do not confront repressive branches or elites directly but rather train popular groups to resist on their own. The state is understood as a space for the mediation of social conflicts, but the unequal power of different state institutions guarantees that the government will primarily serve the interests of elites while legitimating itself as the advocate for the downtrodden. However, the state, through its progressive institutions, absorbs revolutionary energies, co-opting radical intellectuals and grassroots leaders who are disciplined and canalized through the state apparatus. In this way, even those who genuinely fight for the rights of vulnerable communities may still contribute to the reproduction of the status quo.

4

▶▶▶▶▶▶▶▶▶▶▶▶▶ ◀◀◀◀◀◀◀◀◀◀◀◀◀

The Culture of Exclusion

Representations of Indigenous Women Street Vendors in Tijuana

Visitors arriving in the city of Tijuana see groups of women and children vendors sitting on the sides of roads or wandering the streets. Selling candies and crafts or begging, the vendors try to attract the attention of tourists who have just crossed the border to get a glimpse of Mexico. Most of the vendors are migrants from the Mixteca; many of them speak dialects of the Mixtec language and some Spanish. Middle-class tijuanenses usually refer to these women by the pejorative nickname Marías; this expression for rural migrant women who work as domestics or street vendors has been in use in Mexico City since the 1960s (Arizpe 1975). The nickname "María" seems to make reference to the Virgin Mary; the husbands of these women are called Josés after Joseph, the husband of Mary. Those who call these women María and their husbands José may just be giving them a common name to emphasize that they are humble people (aristocratic people in Latin America are distinguished by having several names and an illustrious last name). Thus, there may be an element of class in the nickname. In addition, these women are represented as mothers, but bad mothers rather than good mothers like Mary. Those who call them Marías may be making reference to Catholic gender categories.

The presence of indigenous women and children in Tijuana's tourist center has provoked heated debate among different sectors of local society, including merchants, social scientists, municipal authorities, other members of the middle class, and indigenous vendors themselves. In this chapter, I compare representations of these indigenous street vendors and contrast the image of the Marías with the ways indigenous women see themselves. I do so to analyze the articulations of ethnicity, gender, and class in a particular political-economic context and to suggest how representations of indigenous vendors may naturalize the exclusion of these particular Mixtec women from access to resources and opportunities. Some representations are openly hostile, whereas others discriminate against these women through a form of paternalistic love (Jackman 1994). These different discourses reflect Mexico's ambivalence toward the nation's indigenous peoples.

In each section of the chapter, I first examine the stereotypes put forward by merchants, municipal authorities, and middle-class citizens as reported in the local press. I then compare these representations with the responses of anthropologists and other social scientists, often advocates for indigenous migrants. Finally, I compare both sides of the debate with indigenous women's own thoughts on these topics. The comments of advocates and indigenous women are often shaped as responses to discriminatory stereotypes.

Marisol de la Cadena (1996) has shown how the images and identities of Cuzco's mestizas arise at the interface of different kinds of elite discourses and the everyday struggles and self-understandings of these women. By looking at the contrast between representations and self-understandings, de la Cadena illustrates competing elite and plebeian racial and ethnic definitions. According to de la Cadena (1996, 10), local elites aim to discipline popular groups by imposing on them a fixed racial taxonomy "based on allegedly biologically ascribed attributes that include morality, sexual behavior and education." Meanwhile, common people stress more flexible ethnic identities that rely on culturally and economically achievable differences. Similarly, Colloredo-Mansfeld (1998) contrasts ideas of race in the Ecuadorian Andes that are based on elite fears of contamination by filth and disease, with indigenous ethnic pride. Both de la Cadena and Colloredo-Mansfeld understand imposed and biologized stigma as race, whereas they define celebratory grassroots self-identification as ethnicity.

This chapter builds on de la Cadena's and Colloredo-Mansfeld's work by focusing on the contrast between different kinds of elite and middle-class discourses and grassroots self-identifications to illuminate social struggles on the meanings of difference and inequality. Like de la Cadena and Colloredo-Mansfeld, I show that popular identities are more fluid than are dominant taxonomies, because they allow for a social mobility that dominant images tend to preclude. However, I contend that discriminatory labels do not present themselves in this case in the form of biologized race but rather in the shape of ethnic-cultural identifications. Whereas the Andean elites studied by de la Cadena and Colloredo-Mansfeld used biologized categories, the impact of the Revolution has made it more difficult to find this kind of discourse in Mexico: the 1910 Revolution was led by anthropologists who studied with antiracist scholar Franz Boas, who was a pioneer of cultural relativism. Mexican indigenista anthropologists rejected the biological inferiority of indigenous peoples and started to promote through state institutions, including schools, the concept that Indians and mestizos were separated by cultural differences that could be overcome with education and socioeconomic mobility. This transition from race to culture was reinforced in later decades in an international context in which institutions like the United Nations promoted the discarding of racial thought. Although assumptions about biological race are still held by individuals (see chapter 5), in Mexico it is not considered politically correct to express thoughts that could be interpreted as biological racism.

In spite of this transition from the concept of biological race to culture, I submit that the very concept of indigenous culture, as defined and shaped by some non-Indian academics in Tijuana, has further marginalized indigenous migrants. Characterizing manifestations of poverty as the traditions of this group, some social scientists have interpreted street vending, child labor, and the building of hovels in dangerous urban spaces as cultural choices. I will show how the concept of culture has operated in this particular context to freeze social inequalities. As Lila Abu-Lughod (1991), Walter Benn Michaels (1992), and Visweswaran (1998) have noted, the anthropological concept of culture, which was originally devised to transcend the discriminatory and hierarchical implications of race, can still carry a sense of difference, ultimately racial, that implies hierarchy. Michaels (1992, 683) writes,

It is only if we think that our culture is not only whatever beliefs and practices we actually happen to have but is instead the beliefs and practices that should properly go with the sort of people we happen to be that the fact of something belonging to our culture can count as a reason for doing it. But to think this is to appeal to something that must be beyond culture and that cannot be derived from culture precisely because our sense of which culture is properly ours must be derived from it. This has been the function of race. . . . The modern concept of culture is not, in other words a critique of racism; it is a form of racism.

Michaels goes on to explain that cultural difference, once logically constructed over the concept of race, does not get rid of hierarchy, although statements of hierarchy might be softened, as when the belief that "our culture is better" (meaning North American or Western culture in Michaels's text) is altered for "better for us." Although Michaels shows that the modern concept of culture is based on assumptions of racial difference, he does not explain how "culture" can function as a metaphor for inequality and how the concept of culture can operate as a form of racism. A. Gordon and C. Newfield (1994, 741) have written in a critical response to Michaels's article, "But what is it about cultural identity that is racist? Is it that a certain group . . . deploys cultural identity for its own interests or from its own exclusionary perspective? Or is something wrong with cultural identity itself, an inherent flaw that renders irrelevant historical or political distinctions among different uses? To polarize the issue again, does the problem lye in racist uses or in the appeal to race itself?" I hold that the problem is not only that culture implies race but that culture is deployed and used to stand for and perpetuate social hierarchies. Michaels does not examine whether those who do not belong to the dominant mainstream think, first, that what is constructed as their culture is actually theirs and, second, that their "culture" is better or even "better for them."

The Political Economy of the Debate

Typically, tourists spend a few hours in Tijuana and make purchases that contribute in a modest way to the city's formal and informal economy

(Bringas and Carrillo 1991; Proffitt 1994). Given the kind of tourism attracted to Tijuana, the competition between merchants (*comerciantes establecidos* is the term used in the local press) and street vendors is fierce. Merchants complain that street vendors, especially indigenous women, are unfair competition because they do not have to pay rent, salespeople, or taxes. Therefore, they are able to sell their merchandise at lower prices and still make a profit. Other members of the middle class complain as well of the urban chaos caused by the proliferation of informal street vendors.

Tijuana's merchant elite originated in the early twentieth century, at a time when activities restricted or forbidden in the United States (drinking, alcohol, gambling) were transferred to Tijuana (Bringas and Carrillo 1991; Proffitt 1994). These businesses entered a crisis in the 1930s with the termination of Prohibition in the United States and the establishment of moral policies in Mexico during President Lázaro Cárdenas's government. To overcome the crisis caused by these changes, border merchants were given import-export privileges and a free-trade zone was established in the border. Tijuana's merchants like to trace their origin as a group to the creation of the free-trade zone because they do not want to be associated with "vice" or with the city's black legend. Since the 1970s, the official promotion of tourism in the border region has encouraged the establishment of numerous restaurants and craft shops. Tijuana's merchants run a variety of businesses in the tourist center that target United States visitors, specifically handicraft and clothing shops, restaurants, bars, nightclubs, and pharmacies.[1] Although Tijuana's middle-class citizens also sometimes patronize these businesses, prices are set in U.S. dollars, and U.S. currency is preferred to Mexican pesos.[2]

Municipal authorities have responded with ambivalence to the conflict between merchants and street vendors. Since the early 1980s, to please merchants and the urban middle classes, they have occasionally harassed and prosecuted street vendors. However, they also grant permits to street vendors, allowing them to sell in the tourist center to get political support from this numerous and well-organized group, while charging their organizations a fee to obtain additional revenues. Moreover, municipal authorities have tried to project a good image of their relationship with street vendors because of indigenous peoples' importance to Mexican politics as representatives of national identity and the poor. From this point of view,

little difference exists between the PRI local and state administrations before 1989 and the PAN administrations after 1989, although the parties
question each other over issues related to indigenous street vendors. Before 1989, in order to illustrate his corruption and antidemocratic behavior, the PAN accused the PRI governor of harassing indigenous women
vendors (*Zeta*, May 25–June 1, 1984; June 1–8, 1984; June 8–15, 1984; August
31–September 7, 1984). Since 1989, the PRI and PRD have accused PAN of
social insensitivity and during elections have tried to mobilize networks of
indigenous migrants against their political adversary (*Zeta,* August 19–25,
1994).

Anthropologists and sociologists have been important agents in the
conflict among indigenous women vendors, merchants, and municipal authorities because, in Latin America, intellectuals are often involved in politics and policy design. A trajectory from academia and political activism to
a position with a government institution or, more recently, a nongovernmental organization is common. As advocates of indigenous women vendors, social scientists respond to the stereotypes circulating in the press
and popular opinion. Challenging merchants' and press statements, scholars argue that Mixtec women do not beg and do not damage the city's image. On the contrary, they maintain that indigenous vendors are honest
workers (Clark 1988). Thus, social scientists propose that indigenous
women should be given street-vending permits and allowed to operate in
the tourist center (Clark 1988; Coronado 1994; Millán and Rubio 1992;
Moreno 1988; Velasco 1995).

In 1983, Tijuana's indigenous migrants formed a political organization
called Asociación de Mixtecos Residentes en Tijuana (ASMIRT) [Associa-
tion of Mixtecs Living in Tijuana] under the leadership of Víctor Clark, a
mestizo anthropologist, and a group of indigenous teachers. ASMIRT's
goals were similar to those of an urban social movement: to fight against
police harassment of street vendors, gain street-vending permits for members, and obtain services and infrastructure in neighborhoods where indigenous migrants live (Nagengast and Kearney 1990). Street-vending
permits allowed indigenous vendors to operate without harassment in
public spaces but also organized them in groups that were easily co-opted
by the state and made them vulnerable to extortion by local government
officials. For instance, ASMIRT collaborated with PRI's political opposition

until 1986, when it became fragmented into a number of street vendor and neighborhood organizations that were gradually co-opted by the then ruling party (Millán and Rubio 1992). When the PAN won the state and local elections in 1989, some of these organizations came closer to that party whereas others remained faithful to the PRI. In some cases indigenous organizations had friendly relations with both parties as well as with the PRD (interview by author with ASMIRT leader 1997).

The conflict in Tijuana resembles conflicts between street vendors, merchants, and local authorities elsewhere (Babb 1989; Castañeda 1997; Cross 1998). In all these cases, a sudden proliferation of street vendors, growing opposition to them, and the inability—or unwillingness—of local authorities to deal effectively with the problem can be considered in the context of a deep economic crisis and structural adjustment policies (for example, government downsizing and shrinking government subsidies and public welfare) that force increasing numbers of people into the informal economy.

Anonymous Marías

Merchants and other members of the middle class have constructed indigenous women vendors as anonymous beings by using a common name, María, for all of them. In photographs and illustrations in local newspapers, Marías are depicted in patterned ways, as sitting or standing women surrounded by children. These images remind one of the picturesque types who represented racial and professional categories in nineteenth-century photographs (Poole 1997). An article entitled "Otra vez las 'Marías'" describes indigenous vendors:

> The case of the Mixtec Indian women popularly known as Marías returns to the discussion table. . . . Most citizens in Tijuana believe that Marías make up a particular group of people who beg while they pretend to be street vendors who sell chewing gum, flowers or other merchandise. Marías typically drag their little children by their hands or carry them on their backs in order to elicit the sympathy of the public, especially North American tourists. Their picturesque dress and way of speaking educe humanitarian reactions as well as curiosity in visitors (*El Heraldo*, August 27, 1984).

Other components of the stereotype stand out as well in this quote: Marías are deviants who carry out an illegal activity (begging) while pretending to be vendors; Marías are bad mothers who profit from their children; Marías stand out in the urban landscape because of their ethnicity. Denial of the women's individuality and identity as well as the pejorative connotations of the nickname itself disturb indigenous women. For example, an indigenous woman vendor named Francisca complains that her name changed when she migrated to Mexico City to work as a domestic servant. She says, "I have suffered quite a bit. But that is the way I learned. And, poor little me, they gave me the name María. That is my name there. My employer said, "I am going to call you 'Maria.'" And I said: Yes, Miss, it is fine. That was all I could do." The denial of the individuality of the Other is a widespread characteristic of racism. Scholars have shown that stigmatized racial or ethnic groups are often addressed as representatives of their group and not as individuals (see, for example, Feagin and Vera 1995; Omi and Winant 1986). This example also shows that those in positions of power have the ability to name and shape social identities that, in this case, are officially accepted while privately rejected.

The stereotype of the María assumes that all indigenous migrant women are street vendors. This idea contrasts sharply with their varied work experiences. Among the women I interviewed, all had been agricultural day laborers at some point in their lives, and a few who had completed high school worked as teachers or in white-collar occupations. Women who had completed primary school worked in export-oriented factories, where a primary school diploma is required. Women without a primary education diploma worked as street vendors, and only very recent arrivals begged.

Neither from Here nor There: Marías as Outsiders

Marías are represented as outsiders in relation to urban spaces in Mexico. According to Lourdes Arizpe (1975), in Mexico City before the 1970s it was not considered usual for peasant women dressed as Indians to use public spaces for street vending in the city center or in middle- and upper-class neighborhoods. For that reason, Arizpe notes, indigenous vendors became homogenized as a group under the rubric "las Marías" and were framed as a social problem by state authorities and the middle class. The popular media character *la india María*, who has been at the center of many Mexican film and television comedies since the 1970s, expresses a similar idea. The contrast between an indigenous peasant woman and urban modern Mexico is expected to produce surprise and laughter in the viewing public. However, this character also portrays a changing social reality: the growing number of indigenous migrants who live in Mexican cities. This "racialization" of space (Radcliffe and Westwood 1996)—the idea that indigenous people belong to the countryside and not to the city—has its origins in the colonial legislation and informal discriminatory practices that kept Indians from the city center and assigned them to the countryside (Cope 1994). This colonial construction of Indians as rural is so resilient that it is still dominant in many Latin American countries despite the fact that increasing numbers of indigenous people live and work in cities (Wade 1997).

Similarly, merchants, municipal authorities, and other middle-class citizens do not perceive indigenous women as rightful inhabitants of Tijuana despite a thirty-year-old community of indigenous migrants. A local official noted in the late 1980s, when the indigenous community was eighteen years old, "Yes, they invade the commercial areas of the city and are believed to be a plague" (quoted by Clark 1988, 82). In the early 1980s, municipal authorities, pressured by merchants, attempted to expel indigenous women vendors from Tijuana, forcing them to ride several buses that would take them outside the city and leave them on the route to Guadalajara (Clark 1988). In an interview, the vice president of Tijuana's merchant association defined merchants as the backbone of the urban community and indigenous street vendors as recently arrived people whose intention was to cross to the United States as soon as possible (interview conducted by author with Jose Luis Portillo, July 1997). Although some indigenous migrants do use the city as a temporary base, others have been living in Tijuana for decades and plan to stay. Portillo's statement ignores the fact that many merchants are themselves relatively recent migrants. Likewise, the merchant association president—a native of Veracruz and a Tijuana resident for twenty-eight years—suggested, "Perhaps street vendors are not interested in Tijuana's good because they are not natives of the city or because they have been living in the city for a short time" (*Zeta*, September 22–29 1989). As in the case of indigenous migrants in San

Quintín, the definition of all indigenous migrants as recently arrived people and transitory is often used to deny them rights, such as education, health services, and decent housing (interview conducted by author with INI anthropologist, August 1997). In fact, merchants use this assumption to claim that municipal authorities should favor their interests over those of street vendors, who should be controlled and expelled from the streets. Challenging this, an indigenous migrant leader asserts the right of his community to settle in:

> What we should do is to organize to request housing and services from the government. It does not matter whether we are migrants. Here, under the border, they call us indigenous migrants, and we are. However, they do not acknowledge that we, migrants, are not invading. We are a source of cheap labor for agrarian producers. Our future should be in Baja California. We should fight for a space for migrants. They should forget that we are migrants. We are settled migrants already. (Gonzalo Montiel, quoted by Velasco 1999, 251)

Despite Montiel's request that indigenous migrants be considered settled in Baja California, he still defines them as rural "cheap labor for agrarian producers" even though he himself is an urban leader. As he is challenging a stereotype, he is reproducing other. Perhaps, by representing Indians as a rural labor force he intends to legitimate them and to demonstrate that they are not invaders. Perhaps it might have seemed more difficult to Montiel to show that an Indian in a city is not an invader given dominant beliefs that Indians belong to the countryside. The representation of the Other as an outsider and a newcomer is a form of discrimination used elsewhere. Suzanne Oboler (1995) demonstrates that Latinos in the United States are usually perceived as outsiders and new immigrants despite their centuries- or decades-long residence in U.S. territory. In Tijuana, indigenous migrants are often perceived as outsiders in another kind of space that is defined as white in dominant discourses: the northern region. According to Alonso (1995) and Nugent (1993), the dominant construction of northern Mexican identity was forged by colonists who perceived themselves to be whites struggling against "rebel Indians." Their imagined community (Anderson 1983) excluded northern indigenous groups that were relocated, "pacified," and in some cases, almost completely exterminated. Today, the idea that northerners are white is used to discriminate against immigrants from the south, especially if they are indigenous.

Indigenous women are also represented as outsiders in another way. An article published in *Mexicano* (July 2, 1996) suggests that indigenous vendors betray the Mexican nation because they encourage their children to speak English and prefer U.S. dollars to Mexican pesos. Jaime Ríos, the article's author, quotes an indigenous vendor, María, saying proudly, "Our children are forced by the circumstances to speak Spanish, English, and our mother tongue. They are trilingual children. . . . We have our money in the bank. I have an account in U.S. dollars because I don't like Mexican pesos." María is then harshly criticized by a mestizo vendor who, according to Ríos, works out of need and not out of greed like the Mixtecs. This vendor's name is Guadalupe, a name that resonates with the key Mexican nationalist symbol, the Virgin of Guadalupe. Guadalupe states, "Although they work on the other side [the USA], have brand-new trucks, drink Budweiser, and earn good wages in U.S. dollars, they still send their old women to sell chewing gum and dolls and their children and grandchildren to beg to the gringos. They have a considerable amount of money in the bank. . . . We all are losing due to these folks. They beg out of greed, not out of need" (*Mexicano*, July 2 1996, 7).

In a study of stereotypes of indigenous women street vendors held by merchants, middle-class, and local authorities, Clark (1988, 67) finds that Marías are often accused of speaking English and making good salaries in U.S. dollars while pretending to be poor and ignorant. He quotes a merchant stating, "They should be exiled. They are a shame for Mexico."

It should be noted that merchants claim to be contributing to the nation when they interact with tourists, speak English to them, and accumulate their dollars. They argue that they are bringing in foreign exchange and creating sources of employment (interview conducted by author with José Luis Portillo, July 1997). Tijuana's middle-class citizens usually have accounts in U.S. dollars and send their children to bilingual schools. However, when indigenous people take advantage of the border economy, they are harshly criticized. This discursive strategy presents the interests of mestizos as those of the community, whereas indigenous street vendors' interests are considered selfish and particular. The representation of indigenous women as treacherous sell-outs to a foreign power and tools of colonialism has a precedent in the figure of Malinche, lover of and translator for the Spanish conqueror Hernán Cortés (discussed in Melhuus 1996). It is interesting that Guadalupe, quoted in *Mexicano*, elaborates a critique of capitalism (greed rather than need), which is associated with United States influence, together with a critique of Indians. Is the article implying that Indians do not belong to capitalism but to the subsistence economy? That capitalism, like contact with things North American, is good for some but not for Indians? Or is the author's intention to carry out a nationalist critique of capitalism in general?

In contrast, social science advocates for Mixtec migrants understand indigenous culture as the foundation of Mexican national identity and suggest that preserving and reinforcing this culture ensures the "Mexicanness" of the U.S. border (Clark 1988). They suggest that the right way to preserve indigenous culture is to shield indigenous migrants from contamination by "foreign elements," embodied in tourists and North American groups who donate to poor neighborhoods. The protection proposed by advocates would drastically reduce migrants' income, however.

Both ideas reflect the fear and anxiety felt by the Mexican middle classes about loss of (state and elite) control over indigenous people in a context of border contact and international migration. Merchants and other members of the middle class fear that indigenous women would become "uppity" if they were able to make their living out of foreign resources. Advocates fear the foreign contamination of the nation, a nation that is represented by the indigenous. In both cases the middle classes are allowed to benefit from the economic and cultural opportunities of a border setting, whereas indigenous peoples are not. Until recently, only elites were able to be cosmopolitan and transcend the limits of the state. A fear that this privilege has been extended to new groups might also be involved in the critique.

Indigenous women agree with advocates that they represent the nation. Although ideas of the nation are constructed largely from above and internalized through state rituals, public education, and the media, Radcliffe and Westwood (1996) argue that popular groups are still able to relate to the nation and the national in a variety of ways, even contesting official definitions. Ofelia, a Tijuana street vendor leader, says, "Our people from Oaxaca, we are Mexicans. Why are we despised? I defend my Mexican blood because they abuse my people. I am a legitimate Mexican. I am not racially mixed. I am Mixtec. I defend my rights and my country" (interview by author, August 1997). In contrast with the idea that the mestizo represents the Mexican nation, Ofelia, expressing the internalization of racial categories by indigenous people, argues that the "pure" Indian is more Mexican because she does not carry foreign elements in her blood. This belief does not reflect, however, a popular reworking of the idea of the nation but rather a grassroots selection of one of the available elite nationalisms as represented in the debate between merchants and advocates.

Despite their nationalism, several indigenous women that I interviewed perceive their relationship to North Americans as a friendly one.[3] Ofelia notes, "We love gringos because they support us. We do not want people to steal from the gringos. I love tourism very much." Honoria agrees, "Yes, many gringos are good. All gringos are good. They buy from us and give us money. They let us keep the change. Yes, the gringos treat us well and some of them have defended us." In contrast to the widespread idea in Tijuana that racism is a North American import, indigenous women seem to associate discriminatory behavior more often with Mexican mestizos, such as members of Tijuana's police force, merchants, and bus and taxi drivers. It should be noted that more than approximately half of the tourists who visit Tijuana are Mexican Americans who tend to value Indianness positively as an essential part of their own ethnic identity (Bringas and Carrillo 1991; Oboler 1995). Thus, many are sympathetic to indigenous women, a fact resented by merchants and the middle class who claim, "We have seen some tourists hugging indigenous women or kissing indigenous children. I don't know how they don't feel repugnance, these women are so dirty" (a merchant quoted by Clark 1988, 65).

Bad Mothers, Drunken Fathers

Marías are defined not only as outsiders but also as deviants according to the proper gender roles identified by merchants, authorities, and other middle-class citizens. Indigenous women are often represented in the press as bad mothers who exploit their own children (e.g., *Zeta*, September 22–

29, 1989; *Mexicano*, July 2, 1996). For example, Marcos Levy, president of the Cámara Nacional de Comercio de Tijuana (CANACO) [National Chamber of Commerce of Tijuana], claimed in an interview, "Because many of them bring their little children with them, these kids are exposed to the dangers of a busy avenue like Revolution Avenue. . . . It would help to create a day care, because it is considered a danger for these children to be with their mothers. Besides, at day care, perhaps the children could even learn something (*Zeta*, September 22–29, 1989). The merchant association vice president, Jose Luis Portillo, added, "We don't want ethnic children in Revolution Avenue. These children are exploited. They are rented. These women, the Marías, rent the children" (interview conducted by author with Jose Luis Portillo, July 1997). Similarly, a local female authority in charge of social services informed an indigenous woman who had been arrested for selling without a permit, "I am an authority who is trying to help you. If you need a job we can find a job for you. However, you can't sell with your children. To use children for the purpose of making profits is a crime" (quoted by Clark 1988, 78). In a social context where motherhood is constructed as the very essence of female social identity (Craske 1999), and taking into account that Catholic gender roles emphasize motherhood and represent it symbolically in the Virgin Mary from which Marías get their generic name, to accuse this group of women of being bad mothers effectively dishonors them. These comments also refer to a struggle in the capitalist system that expects poor children to be both objects of social reproduction (accomplished by schools) and objects of production (child labor). According to Tijuana's merchants, indigenous children should be in school instead of working with their mothers. However, the capitalist system in a third world country like Mexico does not provide poor children with the conditions (food, economic and psychological welfare, time) and the resources (schools, pedagogic materials) to be objects of social reproduction. Thus, children are forced to become objects of production. However, their mothers are blamed for profiting from their own children, and these women become scapegoats for processes that they do not control.

To "protect" street children, Tijuana's merchants founded a committee in collaboration with Dirección Integral de la Familia (State Department of Family Issues). Indigenous children working in the streets are picked up and placed in government facilities. This project has been widely criticized in Baja California because children are "protected" only on weekends and holidays, when more tourists visit. Moreover, children are often mistreated in the facilities; at least one child has died while being "protected" within this initiative (Millán and Rubio 1992). The state, which is unable to provide welfare and education for these children, removes them from the streets to favor merchants business.

Unlike merchants, social scientists claim that indigenous women prefer to work in the informal sector because the flexible schedule allows them to carry out their household chores more efficiently and to take better care of their children (Coronado 1994; Millán and Rubio 1992; Velasco 1995). Some add that child labor is an indigenous tradition that will, perhaps, disappear when indigenous migrants realize the importance of education. Millán and Rubio (1992, 11) state, "Indigenous vendors' children wander the city working with their parents or begging. This problem is particularly delicate . . . because the ethnic and cultural characteristics of migrants require the integration of children to the family's economy." Thus, advocates interpret street vending in the company of children as a choice or a cultural tradition instead of a necessity. This is a clear example of social inequality being naturalized when interpreted as culture.

Indigenous women neither share the perception that they are bad mothers nor think that child labor is a tradition in their community. First, they perceive separation from their children as a form of punishment that has convinced many to discontinue their street-vending activities. Second, they perceive child labor, including their own work when they were children, as an unfortunate consequence of economic need and not an ethnic custom. Although the women feel that street vending is an honest job, they would like their children to get a formal education and be able to practice a profession.

In press articles reflecting merchants' viewpoints, Mixtec men are represented as bad husbands and parents who lack masculinity because they are unable to support their families. It is believed that if women and children have to work, it is because men are drunken vagrants. The president of Tijuana's National Chamber of Commerce noted that Tijuana's city hall offered one hundred construction jobs to Mixtec men, and none of them showed up. "We don't know what is happening. Perhaps it is their tradition that only the women work," he said, using the concept of "tradition" sarcastically to suggest that Mixtec men might be using "tradition" to justify their inability to provide for their families (*Zeta*, September 22–29, 1989). After interviewing merchants, authorities, and middle-class citizens, Victor Clark (1988) found that one of the most commonly held stereotypes of indigenous women vendors is that they are exploited by their husbands. One interviewee stated, "Their husbands send them to work and they don't do anything. They just spend their time drinking" (Clark 1988, 71). As noted in chapter 1, Mixtec men work in commercial agriculture, construction, and services in the north of Mexico and in the United States, but because their remittances are not necessarily sufficient to support their families, women's and children's work is essential (Velasco 1995). Moreover, as many have observed, the ideal of the male breadwinner and the female housewife is a middle-class model and a luxury that the working classes have only occasionally been able to afford (see, for example, Fernández-Kelly 1983; Tilly and Scott 1978).

It is interesting to note that, despite the stereotype of the drunken husband, migrant women are more often represented as treacherous than men. Perhaps this happens because women compete economically with the middle classes in the tourist center of the city, whereas indigenous men occupy what the middle classes consider their proper place in low-wage occupations in construction, commercial agriculture, and ice cream vending in poor neighborhoods where fewer gains can be made. They are not constructed as deviants in their own right, but only take on that identity because they allow their wives to work.

Paternalism and Ambivalence

Merchants and the middle class are not always hostile toward indigenous people. On the contrary, they are often paternalistic and ambivalent. Merchants are reluctant to express open hostility toward indigenous women because they do not want to be accused of bigotry in a context in which indigenous peoples are symbolically protected by post-Revolutionary populism (Dietz 1995). For that reason, merchants argue that by expelling indigenous vendors from the streets they wish to shield them and their children from dangerous or unrewarding conditions. Marcos Levy of the National Chamber of Commerce argues, "[T]hese people are workers who don't have the benefits that they would enjoy in a formal business" (*Zeta*, September 22–29, 1989). Merchants also ask the government to offer employment alternatives to women and their families.

Some of these tensions are also reflected in the design of urban space dedicated to tourism. On Tijuana's main street, Revolution Avenue, merchants created a stereotypical Mexico to attract tourism. It is a colorful Mexico populated by mariachis where fiestas are celebrated twenty-four hours a day and cheap alcohol is readily available. Merchants adorn this tourist Mexico with some indigenista touches; for example, a pre-Hispanic corridor that was under construction when I was doing fieldwork features imitations of the archaeological remains of Mexico's great ancient civilizations. Here the merchants sell indigenous crafts and have adopted an Aztec logo as the symbol of the merchant association. However, merchants feel that there should be no space for indigenous women vendors in their artificial Mexico, because, according to them, tourists should not be bothered by the nation's "social problems." We have here two constructions of the Indian: the ancient indigenous civilizations and their survival in the form of crafts are used as markers of national identity and as a commodity for tourist consumption, whereas the contemporary Indian is understood as a social problem (Dietz 1995; Friedlander 1975).

The Culture of Exclusion

While defending the right of indigenous women to work in public spaces, some intellectuals unintentionally use arguments based on understandings of culture that tend to naturalize and romanticize the marginal position of indigenous women in urban labor markets. Some scholars perceive informal street vending as an appropriate activity for indigenous women because it is part of their tradition (Millán and Rubio 1992; Velasco 1995), it allows indigenous migrants to work with their *paisanos* (people from their own town), and it reinforces ethnic ties (Coronado 1994). In this way, the necessity for indigenous women to work on the streets because they lack better opportunities becomes what local intellectuals call a "cultural choice." According to Coronado (1994, 9), "Street vending is a tradition in their community and it is not a new form of subsistence. This employment is not a way of combating unemployment; rather it has been a way of life for these women." Similarly Velasco (1995, 56–57) argues, "Commerce is economically, politically and socially important not only in the Mixteca region but in the whole state of Oaxaca. A complex market system has existed for centuries to secure the survival of indigenous groups. For these reasons, Mixtec women are endowed with a cultural training for commerce. . . . Commerce as a cultural alternative has been facilitated by the expansion of tourism in this city [Tijuana]."

Other features associated with the poverty of indigenous migrants are explained through the concept of culture. Building homes in marginal neighborhoods on dangerous hills and in riverbeds where landslides and flooding are common is also defined as a "cultural choice" rather than a consequence of the lack of access to formal housing markets. According to Moreno (1988, 101), "The geography of the place where the neighborhood is located forces them to build their houses in riverbeds and on hills. There, Mixtecs feel good because it reminds them, many of them, of the physical characteristics of their hometown."

Some advocates argue that indigenous "culture" must be preserved by segregating indigenous migrants from outside influences, even when these influences open economic opportunities for them, as in the case of contact with tourists and North American aid groups. In an article in *El Heraldo*, Clark suggests that the anthropologist, as a specialist on "culture," as well as the indigenous bilingual teacher, are the only professionals who should interact with and represent indigenous migrants. Clark states, "It is necessary to preserve their [indigenous] culture and protect them from any kind of religious or political contamination. Certainly the anthropologist and the teacher are agents of change and, for that reason, we should defend the Marías whenever it is needed. I personally believe that the Indian is the raw material for the anthropologist and that rather than study her, we should help her and guide her" (*El Heraldo*, September 5, 1984, 1a and 6a). Anthropologists assume a paternalistic attitude when they present themselves as the privileged representatives of indigenous migrants whom they will guide and protect. I would suggest that this form of paternalism resembles colonial understandings of Indians as legal minors who ought to be represented by mestizo advocates such as government officials, priests, and politicians.[4]

The belief that segregation is the best way to protect Indians also

shows the legacy of colonial arrangements. After the early colonial decima-
tion of indigenous population, the Spanish crown congregated indigenous
people in separate communities, *Repúblicas de Indios*, under crown and
church guidance partly to curb colonists' abuse but also to facilitate administration and taxation (Wolf 1982). This construction of Indians as minors who should be segregated for their own protection even if it means
exclusion from societal resources is very similar to the approach of the anthropologist and director of the Department of Popular Cultures that I described in chapter 3.

In contrast to Clark's assumption that they must be guided, indigenous women emphasize their own agency and their involvement in politics. Ofelia, the street vendor leader, explains that when she arrived in
Tijuana in the 1960s she fought against the authorities, demanding respect
for her people. Now things have changed, according to her, and she has
good relationships with all three levels of government, which at the time of
our conversation were controlled by different political parties. Thanks to
her political work, she obtained street-vending permits for the women of
her organization and resources from the National Solidarity Program to
build street-vending carts to exhibit their merchandise. She follows a
clientelistic logic in her political work: "If the government gives us things,
we have to help the government," she says.

Indigenous women's understanding of ethnicity is also different from
that of advocates. Some women wish their children to integrate into mestizo society so the children will be spared the discrimination their parents
have suffered. Ofelia says, "It is not necessary that they speak Mixtec. The
Mixtec language does not help them much. Spanish and English are more
helpful. They should not live with our race any more. They should live with
other people." Honoria, another street vendor, agrees: "The truth is that
one suffers a lot because here, they say that they are mestizos, and they
insult us. And if the children did not understand [Spanish] they would be
miserable." Other women want their children to keep the Mixtec language
and identity, but not at the expense of getting a formal education and other
opportunities offered by mainstream society. Ninfa, for example, says, "I
would not like them to lose our language, because we are Mixtecs, and I
would like them to also speak Mixtec. When they arrive in the city, many
people do not want to remember their origin. I believe that it is not good to

forget who we are. I would like my children to study. I would like my children to be good students, and I will fight so they go to school." Unlike the director of the Department of Popular Cultures, Ninfa does not see a contradiction between preserving her culture and having access to formal education. Ninfa is the daughter and sister of political leaders in the community. During fieldwork, I observed that indigenous leaders tended to favor the preservation of their language and culture, whereas most grassroots migrants preferred assimilation.

Conclusion

Omi and Winant (1986, 72) argue that to identify a social project as discriminatory, one must demonstrate the link between essentialist representations and social structures of domination. Such a link might be revealed in efforts to protect dominant interests through the construction of racial or ethnic categories. By essentialist representations I mean the belief that a bounded group of people is endowed with a fixed set of traits that originates in the remote past and is not likely to change in the near future. In the case discussed here, representations of indigenous women vendors as outsiders from different social spaces—such as the city, northern Mexico, and the nation—and the depiction of merchants and the middle classes as the backbone of these imagined communities (Anderson 1983) are used to pressure municipal authorities to expel vendor women from the city's economic center. Moreover, the representations of indigenous women and men as deviants from middle-class gender norms reinforces the idea that they are undeserving poor whose interests should not be considered. Karen Brodkin (1998, 246) has noted that in the case of the United States assumed deviance from gender roles as defined by the mainstream has been used to exclude nonwhite people from full citizenship rights: "An important set of popular and scientific discourses attended to by this literature is the variety of ways that non-white and off-white women and men are represented, namely as beings who lack the manly and feminine temperaments that were requisites for full membership in the body politic and social."

Advocates for indigenous women defend their right to use public spaces. However, when they do so, they transform what I would call desperate socioeconomic problems into cultural and gender choices, as if indigenous women like it that way. These advocates also suggest that the way to protect indigenous culture is to exclude Mixtec migrants from opportunities in the border economy. Thus, the concept of culture is used to freeze a particular socioeconomic position as well as exclude a group of people from access to available resources. Michael Kearney (1988) has argued that Mixtec migrants tend to respond to discrimination in the north of Mexico by reinforcing their ethnic consciousness and organization. My findings suggest that there are other possible responses to racism. Some grassroots migrants, especially those who do not hold community leadership positions, wish to overcome discrimination through attempts to integrate into the mainstream.

I have shown how the exclusion of indigenous women from resources and opportunities is often framed as a form of protection and love for them and/or their children. A focus on paternalism is important to the understanding of such discourses. Advocates and merchants use paternalistic arguments for different reasons, however. With some similarity to the case of San Quintín, advocates in Tijuana draw from colonial understandings of Indians as innocent children who must be protected and represented; indigenous people are perceived by their advocates as likeable but not equal. Merchants, on the other hand, may feel the need to use paternalistic arguments because open hostility against indigenous peoples is not easily accepted in post-Revolutionary Mexico or may reveal their own ambivalent feelings toward the nation's Indians.

Finally, I would like to use the case discussed here to reflect on the debate about the anthropological concept of culture. Edward Fischer (1999, 473) argues that "despite its general disrepute within the academy, an essentialist view of culture underwrites many contemporary ethnic movements the world over" and that "antiessentialist constructivism has itself become the target of recent subaltern critiques coming both from within the academy and from the subjects of anthropological inquiry." I find two problems in these statements. First, Fischer seems to assume that most subaltern individuals and groups wish and choose to understand themselves in essentialist terms. Second, and more important, he does not ask why this happens in some instances. I have shown that Tijuana's grassroots indigenous migrants prefer a more fluid understanding of ethnicity because it opens for them the opportunity for social mobility. However, Mixtecs may strategically use essentialist ideas that, we should remember, are not of their own creation. For example, they may claim that they are "the real Mexicans" if it helps them gain respect. Do subaltern groups perhaps take advantage of essentialism to gain legitimacy from audiences who will listen to them only if they assume these stereotyped images? Or are the voices of their advocates and those indigenous leaders influenced by them mistaken for the voices of the grassroots?

This case study shows that the concept of culture, as shaped by some Mexican academics, tends to freeze the socioeconomic inequality between those labeled as Indians and mainstream society defined as mestizo. This finding resembles Lila Abu-Lughod's (1991) critique of the anthropological uses of the concept of culture. Unlike the earlier concept of race as it was understood in the nineteenth and early twentieth centuries, the concept of culture theoretically allows for change (culture can change and be learned) and eludes hierarchy (cultures are expected to be different but not necessarily superior or inferior). However, on occasion, culture operates in anthropological discourse to enforce and freeze hierarchical differences. This happens, according to Abu-Lughod, because the very discipline of anthropology is based on the ongoing construction of an opposition between the Western self and the non-Western other in a context of Western domination. For these reasons, Abu-Lughod suggests that we should work against culture, especially as it functions to distinguish cultures.

However, in this chapter I have also tried to approach culture in a different way. Following the work of Poole (1997), Roseberry (1994), Wade (1998), and others, I analyze culture as a set of discourses, images, and ideas that emerges in the context of particular social struggles and political-economic processes and is diffused through particular means of cultural production, such as the press and the merchant association. Therefore, I do not claim, as Abu-Lughod (1991) does, that anthropologists should reject altogether the concept of culture. But, I do argue that we must be aware of the discriminatory effects of some of its uses.

5

▶▶▶▶▶▶▶▶▶▶▶▶▶◀◀◀◀◀◀◀◀◀◀◀◀◀

Race, Maternalism, and Community Development

We visited the community twice a week. The director of our development team, an elegant upper-class woman named Elena, drove us to the neighborhood in a sports utility vehicle with the name of the sponsoring institution printed on both sides. Our group was made up of the director, who had studied social work, a psychologist, a lawyer, several college students fulfilling the community service that is required to graduate from Mexican universities, and an anthropologist (myself). Once in a while, a medical student, also fulfilling obligatory community service, and a nurse joined the group to vaccinate community children and provide checkups for them. Elena and one of the students, the child of a personal friend of hers, were from Mexico City and belonged to the national elite. The other team members, with the exception of myself, were from the north of Mexico and were middle-class or lower-middle-class women.

To get to the community, we had to cross the city of Tijuana. We traveled from the elegant area, where the research center for which we worked was located, to the eastern outskirts of the city, where poor neighborhoods melted into the desert landscape. Ironically, the name of the community where we worked was Valle Verde (Green Valley). Shacks made of scraps and a few unfinished two-story brick buildings flanked Valle Verde's dry and dusty unpaved streets. During my fieldwork, the neighborhood still lacked running water and drainage. Its inhabitants were a mixture of poor indigenous (most of them Mixtec) and mestizo migrants who had been relocated by the government when they lost their feeble homes in a period of catastrophic rains in 1993. Our program's aim was to target only the indigenous migrant population, although in practice we worked with both groups because Elena did not want to discriminate. Although it was not the program's original intention, we ended up working with women, probably because the development team was made up exclusively of women (with the exception of the medical student who came to the neighborhood only once in a while and was not really integrated into the team). Community men did not join our program regularly because they perceived it as "a ladies' thing" (I heard this comment a few times) or because they were working somewhere else on the mornings we visited. Men joined us, however, during some special celebrations and requested help from us with bureaucratic chores.

When we arrived in the community, Elena stopped the vehicle frequently to chat with the indigenous residents. Typically, she commanded them from a distance to come near us. She did not step out of the vehicle or remove her designer sunglasses. The shiny white SUV contrasted with the poverty of the neighborhood. The indigenous residents complied with Elena's command shyly, taking off their hats if they were men,[1] and looking toward the floor. Then, the director changed her tone of voice from authoritarian to the mellow one that is often used with little children. She asked them questions about their jobs, their health, and their families. She proudly displayed her knowledge of the community. They replied to her questions and blushed if they thought their answers would not satisfy her. When Elena was not satisfied by an answer, she would reprimand them shaking her hand and imitating the act of spanking. Then, indigenous migrants asked her for help in processing an official document, getting a badly needed medicine for a sick child, or even obtaining a visa to cross to the United States. It is interesting that indigenous migrants thought that our power to get things for them was greater than it really was. For example, as a Mexican private organization, we had no influence on the Immigration and Naturalization Service of the United States. The rest of the team remained silent while these interactions took place, reflecting a general dynamic in which the director took the initiative and the other members of the team either collaborated or silently resisted but did not dare to challenge her in public.

This kind of interaction, which evokes traditional paternalistic or, better, maternalistic interethnic and interclass relations in Latin America, is not what supporters of nongovernmental organizations (NGOs) would associate with the work of these agencies.[2] Nongovernmental organizations started to play an important role in Latin America in the 1970s. Many originated in the left or prodemocracy groups that struggled against authoritarian governments and human rights abuses. These organizations proliferated and changed in the 1980s, a period of transition to democracy and structural reforms. As the social functions of the state were reduced to balance the public budget according to structural adjustment policies, international funds became available to private organizations that replaced the state as providers of social services. NGOs played a key role to diminish the negative impact of the reforms. Many on both the right and the left praised NGOs in the 1980s, either as symbols of privatization and antistate philosophy or as the way to a new utopia when hopes for a sweeping socialist revolution declined with the fall of the Soviet block (Arellano López and Petras 1994). Critiques of NGO–led development started to appear in the 1990s, as scholars began to study the concrete practices and the impact of these organizations. A growing literature has questioned the ability of NGOs to promote democratization, represent the interests of the poor, and address their needs (see, for example, Abramson 1999; Arellano López and Petras 1994; Bretón 2001; Delpino and Pásara 1991; Gideon 1998; Gill 1997). Advocates still perceive NGOs as efficient, flexible, and democratic organizations able to strengthen civil society, facilitate grassroots political participation, and provide economic opportunities for the poor—especially in contrast to the inefficiency and authoritarianism associated with the state apparatus in developing countries (Cornia, Jolly, and Steward 1987; Queisser, Larrañaga and Panadeiros 1993; Uphoff 1993). Critics, however, argue that a number of NGOs, especially those founded after the 1980s to tap international resources, are prone to corruption and tend to manipulate popular groups into becoming clients instead of citizens when they foster dependent and exclusive[3] relationships with target populations (Arellano and Petras 1994; Gideon 1998; Gill 1997). These critical scholars build on earlier path-breaking works that started to examine the relationships between development and power, between sponsors and recipients of development (Western and non-Western countries respectively), and between agents of development and target populations (Escobar 1995;

Ferguson 1990). These works were inspired by Michel Foucault's emphasis on how discourses and institutions shape subjects and are embedded in power relations.

In this chapter, I will focus on a Mexican NGO in which I did participant observation in the year 1996–1997. My main focus is the role played by this particular NGO in overcoming or reproducing ethnic and class boundaries.[4] I will use this case to discuss some problems raised by the critical literature on development: How is the work of nongovernmental organizations shaped and limited by the different ethnic and class backgrounds of development professionals and target populations (Arellano and Petras 1994; Delpino and Pásara 1991)? How do assumptions of development and democratization in Europe and the United States interact with local cultural interpretations of progress and local sets of social relations (Abramson 1999)? Although these critical authors have dealt with these issues in studies that survey a number of organizations in a geographical area of the world, more work needs to be done to explore these questions in the context of everyday interactions between development workers and target populations. This ethnographic and cultural approach to NGOs has been growing in recent years; examples include Abramson (1999), Bretón (2001), and Occhipinti (2003). An analysis of everyday interactions can help us better understand the ways in which NGOs promote or hinder democratization.

Building on the work of Arturo Escobar (1995), I study the relationship between development and power using the ethnographic method. However, Escobar conceives development as a relationship in which the West exercises power over non-Western countries, a continuation of the colonial relationship by other means once colonialism ended. He is basically right, but he forgets the participation of non-Western elites, middle classes, and states in development practices. Neither colonialism nor development is a form of power that confronts geographical blocks in any simple way. Both phenomena have benefited certain groups within each block. In the same way that Latin American, Asian, and African elites and middle classes collaborated with colonialism and benefited from it, other elites participate and benefit from development or are even created by development itself (Abramson 1999). For instance, NGOs have been identified as important sources of employment for the Latin American upper-middle and middle classes since the 1980s (Arellano and Petras 1994). Unlike Escobar (1995), Ferguson (1990) and Abramson (1999) emphasize the role of non-Western social actors and local cultural interpretations in development work.

The relationship between elites, middle classes, and indigenous and mestizo migrants at the Mexican border, and particularly the effect of this relationship on ethnic identities and boundaries, is also the focus of this chapter. Despite the fact that Laura Nader (1969) encouraged anthropologists to "study up" in the early 1970s to pursue an ethical concern with the exercise of power in society, the anthropological record on elites is still limited (Shore and Nugent 2002). This situation is due in part to the elitist and colonial tradition of a discipline that has specialized in "studying down." The methodological problems of studying elites should be added to this resilient tradition. According to Cris Shore, elites are by definition groups who are able to control their own self-representation and who are shielded from public scrutiny. I was able to have access to the elite woman discussed in this chapter because I worked with her and because my Iberian background and degree from a United States university gave me enough elite status to be able to interview her and interact with her. Although she is only one individual, after comparing her trajectory with more general works on Mexican elites (Adler Lomnitz and Pérez Lizaur 1987; Gledhill 2002), I show that she is representative of the worldview and practices of her class and that we can learn from her about how Mexican upper classes approach indigenous people and the poor.

The study of the relationship between elites and subordinate groups (ethnic groups, the poor), in this case through development work, is important to an understanding of elite identity because it is in part constituted through an elaboration of the difference between the privileged and the underprivileged as well as through the particular way elites relate to subordinates (Jackman 1994). Simultaneously, the contact between the powerful and the disempowered in the context of development contributes to provide elite groups with a benign image in order to help build popular consent to their rule (although this consent could be fragile as this chapter will show later). This is what Antonio Gramsci (1971) called hegemony and Abner Cohen (1981) named elite cultivation of "universalism," a strategy to convince the majority that elites represent wider interests and to legitimate elite rule. Adler Lomnitz and Pérez Lizaur (1987) have discussed the role of women in the maintenance of elite networks and rituals that are key to consolidating the economic and political power of the upper classes. Women also play a pivotal role in the articulation of elite relationships with subordinate groups (Adler Lomnitz and Pérez Lizaur 1987; Weiner 1986; Whisnant 1983). As these authors spell out, social concern has historically been constructed as part of upper-class female personhood.

The Program

The community development program where I did participant observation was founded by a Mexican research center in 1994 to address the problems of migrants to the border region and to defend their human rights. The program carried out a number of activities. It recorded and published human rights violations against migrants by Mexican or United States authorities; it connected migrants with public or private organizations that could help them; and it had a project of direct assistance to indigenous migrants in a neighborhood in Tijuana. I will concentrate here on the project of direct assistance to the indigenous migrant community. The project carried out health campaigns, taught reading and writing to adults, provided indigenous migrants with official documents, such as birth certificates, and created a firm that offered the labor force of Mixtec women access to transnational and national capital for assembly tasks.

The research center was an autonomous institution that depended on the Department of Public Education and was financed in part by the Mexican government and in part by international foundations. When he created the community development program and another program that focused on the enhancement of the urban environment, one of the aims of Ramón, the director of the research center, was to improve his relations with the local community. In an internal publication, he noted that the Tijuana Group (an association of influential people in the city) demanded the disappearance of the research center because they thought that it conducted studies that damaged the image of Tijuana and the local economy. The director responded by emphasizing the academic reputation of the center and its beneficial impact on local society, particularly through its human rights and community development program.

Mixtec migrants were perceived by Ramón as the poorest and most vulnerable among the migrants and were chosen for that reason. It was not their ethnicity but their vulnerability that interested him, although both traits are closely linked at the Mexican border. The population that the community development program helped was vulnerable for three reasons. As indigenous people they were defined as "the poorest among the poor," an expression popularized in the mid-1990s by such government institutions as the National Solidarity Program and the National Indigenist Institute (Fox 1994). The community development program was addressed to recently arrived indigenous women and children from the state of Guerrero who begged or sold candies and handicrafts in the streets and were considered a social problem by merchants and other members of the middle class.

However, Valle Verde residents did not necessarily see their Mixtec neighbors as the poorest and most vulnerable among them. Valle Verde's mestizos claimed that Mixtecs had better houses, savings, and other assets than they did. This impression could be explained in part by resentment that indigenous people had any property, as they were expected to be poor. According to the mestizos whom I interviewed in the neighborhood, the reason for the Mixtecs' relative prosperity was the fact that they were willing to perform tasks that mestizos considered demeaning, such as begging or becoming day laborers. Many of the mestizos in the neighborhood worked in maquiladoras (export-oriented industries) or were unemployed or underemployed. Given this situation, the Salesians, a Catholic religious organization, created workshops to teach neighborhood mestizos to become artisans or independent producers.[5]

I observed that many Mixtecs were building two-story brick houses that were considered signs of upward mobility in the neighborhood, whereas many migrant mestizos lived in fragile houses made from scraps. Many of the neighborhood grocery stores also belonged to Mixtecs. Another reason for the relative prosperity of some Mixtec families was that a number of Mixtec men had been granted visas to work in the United States under the Immigration Regularization and Control Act (IRCA), an immigration law passed in 1986 that had contradictory effects on immigrants: it granted an amnesty to those who had been in the United States for some time but restricted the entrance of newcomers. Some of the Mixtec men who had received visas chose to live in Tijuana and commute daily to the other side of the border to work as gardeners, construction workers, or day laborers (Young 1994). Mixtecs rather than mestizos benefited from IRCA because they had been the preferred labor force in commercial agriculture in the U.S. Southwest for decades and already resided in the neighboring country.

In articles in local and national newspapers and internal publications, the research center's director presented the community development project as a grassroots initiative and a participatory experience. He emphasized that the program activities responded to the concerns and needs of the community and explained that the program was not paternalistic, because it focused on the education of Mixtec women so that they would be able to prosper by themselves and become independent. He wrote that Tijuana's indigenous women

> will lead a process that will transform them from beggars into businesswomen. There is still a long way to go before this transformation is understood by all those whose prejudices preclude them from accepting as possible and legitimate that a group of indigenous women act in a role that local racism can not even imagine. The main obstacle hindering Mixtec women from becoming real businesswomen is neither their low level of education nor their poverty. The main obstacle are the prejudices, sexism, and racism of those around them and of those with whom they must interact in order to become permanent actors in something as abstract, but also as humanly constituted, as what we call the market.

However, the representation of the program as a grassroots, participatory project often contrasted with the prominent role many of those same publications gave to the sponsoring institution and the social workers in order to enhance the image of the research center.

Elena, the director of the community development program, envisioned her initiative as an attempt to provide jobs for indigenous women in their own neighborhood and thus encourage them to discontinue their informal activities. It was a way to solve what the authorities and the local middle class perceived as a social problem. Perhaps because she was married to a man who owned maquiladora industries on the Mexican side of the border, Elena conceived the idea of organizing a cooperative that offered the labor of indigenous women to national and transnational capitalists for industrial assembly tasks. This idea was innovative because, as I learned from informal conversations with middle- and upper-middle-class tijuanenses, indigenous people were locally perceived as good agricultural workers or domestic servants, but not as prospective industrial laborers. Export-oriented factories required their workers to be fluent in Spanish and to have literacy skills, an elementary school diploma, and official identity papers, such as birth certificates and proof of participating in social security. Most indigenous women (and men) did not possess these requirements. Many were illiterate or had not had the opportunity to complete primary education. In their communities of origin, everybody knew everybody else and, as a result of official negligence, they did not register themselves with the state. This became a problem when they migrated, became anonymous citizens, and were required to have official documentation.

Our program aimed to teach indigenous women Spanish, reading, writing, and other skills necessary to get elementary school diplomas, which were granted to them after taking an exam with the Instituto Nacional de Educación de Adultos (INEA) [National Institute for Adult Education], a governmental institution with which our program collaborated. In addition, we processed birth certificates for indigenous migrants in collaboration with the National Indigenist Institute, an institution that had a campaign to promote the registration of indigenous migrants. An additional service of our program was the celebration of collective weddings to regularize the informal unions that were characteristic in the neighborhood. Some at the research center interpreted this service as an attempt to moralize these women, an interpretation supported by the fact that the official of the civil registry of Tijuana gave a speech at one of the collective weddings explaining to indigenous migrants that "marriage was the moral basis for the family." Elena responded to these critiques by arguing that the regularization of marital relationships would protect the women from abuse and abandonment and would secure their economic rights in the family.

Looking at the activities of the program as a whole, Elena's aim seemed to be the transformation of these migrant women of peasant origin into an employable, disciplined, and, perhaps, moral urban industrial labor force. An influential local economist and expert on export-producing zones characterized this task as unrealistic given what he assumed were the limitations of these indigenous women. Moreover, what we may perceive from outside as the utilitarian goal of making migrant women employable in the city's economy was also perceived by Elena's husband and other border industrialists as idealistic and utopian. Again, according to these businessmen, indigenous women were not prepared to become urban proletarians, a category that required a "degree of sophistication" that these women allegedly lacked. The pamphlets addressed to prospective industrial employers differed from the discourse of the president of the research center and were closer to Elena's view. Elena requested help from a firm of United States market consultants that specialized in United States–Mexico commercial relations to create a promotional campaign for the cooperative. These documents, written in Spanish and translated into English, or written in English and translated into Spanish, emphasized the dexterity and docility of Mixtec workers and the low wages that they would be willing to accept in exchange for their work ("Programa de Derechos Humanos. Introducción a Emmix," promotional pamphlet).

The documents asserted, "Both men and women from this ethnic group have amazing skills for manual work because in their region of origin they produce palm hats and other crafts." The pamphlets assured their target audience that Indians would be docile workers: "One of the advantages of working with this group is that between this people there are strong family ties that make them cohesive and collaborative. The mothers, particularly, have expressed their interest in working." The documents continued, "Because this is a company created for the benefit of its own workers, it will not be affected by labor problems." The cooperative offered "an abundant and docile labor force, loyal to its own company, without turn-over and other problems that commonly affect other maquila operations." Finally, the cooperative provided "hourly labor costs similar to local wages, which are among the lowest in the Pacific Rim." These pamphlets tried to convince employers that the migrants' ethnicity would make them ideal members of the urban proletariat. Indianness was interpreted in the documents to represent, among other attributes, dexterity resulting from a tradition of craftsmanship that, in the words of Ramón, "indigenous

women seem to carry in their genes." Ethnicity also brought with it community cohesion that would make these workers more docile than those
with individualistic aspirations. This association of Indianness with docility resembled images of day laborers in San Quintín. The romantic equa-
tion of ethnicity with dexterity and community harmony and the idea that
these qualities could make people ideal industrial workers seem to have
originated with the North American consultants more than in the Mexican
development workers.

The ideas of Ramón, the director of the research center, and Elena, the
director of the community development project, had something in common: both wanted to improve the lot of indigenous women through the
market, either as independent entrepreneurs or as ideal workers. From
this point of view, this was a "neoliberal" NGO, with a different culture
than other NGOs, which originated on the left. Ramón emphasized participation and self-sufficiency, and Elena highlighted obedience, reliability,
and willingness to work hard for low wages. Interestingly, the idea that indigenous women were docile contrasted with the reality of the long history
of conflict between indigenous women street vendors and Tijuana's local
authorities and middle classes. This contrast between discursively constructed docility and a history of activism is also at play in the representation of San Quintín's indigenous day laborers as docile and naïve in spite of
their long history of unionization (see chapter 2). Ramón and Elena addressed different publics. Whereas Ramón spoke to the local community,
the academic community, academic foundations, the Mexican government, and so on, Elena spoke to employers and wished to change the image
the industrial bourgeoisie had of these indigenous women.

Development Workers

To understand Elena's approach to community development and the indigenous migrant community better, it is important to take into account her
class background and worldview, particularly in relation to social hierarchies. Her father came from an old aristocratic family of landowners from
an agriculturally rich northern state. They lost their lands and gold and
silver mines after the Mexican Revolution of 1910 and moved to Mexico City
to escape revolutionary violence. Elena claimed in an interview that ac-

cording to property titles preserved by a cousin, family haciendas covered about half of the state's territory and included many towns. After they lost their properties and social status, her father's family had a hard time in Mexico City. For example, her aunts could not marry and had to work as companions to rich people. According to Elena, her father's family was very conservative. They were faithful supporters of the Porfirio Díaz dictatorship. They were also very religious, to the point that her aunts and other family members were involved in the late 1920s in the Cristero rebellion, an uprising in which the clergy, part of the elites, and popular groups joined forces against the anticlerical laws of the Revolutionary government. Elena's father met her mother in Paris, where he was in exile for several years after the Cristero revolt. Unlike Elena's father, Elena's mother came from a family that made its fortune after the Revolution. Elena's maternal grandfather started a coal business during the Revolution and prospered with real estate developments when things settled down. According to Elena, her mother's family was very progressive, supportive of secularization and social reform, and able to take advantage of the sweeping transformations that were taking place in post-Revolutionary Mexico. Marriage between the two families allowed for the reproduction of the pre-Revolutionary elite as well as for the symbolic reinforcement of the post-Revolutionary bourgeoisie through its connection with earlier aristocratic groups. Elena, for her part, married a prosperous businessman who had investments in export-oriented factories at the border and was a member of the board of directors of a powerful firm that exported Mexican canned foods to the United States. Elena was therefore related to all the interrelated social groups that have dominated Mexico from colonial times to the present: the landed aristocracy, the revolutionary bourgeoisie, and those who profit today from neoliberal free trade policies. The history that Elena detailed in a long interview with me matches the general trajectory of Mexican elites discussed by Adler Lomnitz and Pérez Lizaur (1987) and Gledhill (2002).

Elena lived in the United States; why did she bother to cross the border daily and visit Tijuana where she worked with poor indigenous and mestizo migrants whose problems were difficult to resolve? According to Elena, her vocation for social work originated from diverse sources. The first component was the social sensitivity of her mother, a historical attribute of upper-class female personhood in Latin America and elsewhere (Adler Lomnitz and Pérez Lizaur 1987; Weiner 1986; Whisnant 1983). The construction of social concern as a female domain originates in the association of care work in the family, and by extension in society, with women (Feder Kittay and Feder 2002). In addition, upper-class women have historically provided their group with a "universalistic" reputation, that is, the idea that the elite represents wider interests (Cohen 1981), and have smoothed the relationships between elites and subordinate groups in cases of extreme exploitation. For example, Marli Weiner (1986) discusses how plantation mistresses were in charge of the care and protection of the slaves in the antebellum United States South. In other words, maternalism has historically been an upper-class female duty. The social sensitivity of Elena's mother also resonated with the Revolutionary tradition. According to Elena, her mother was a very progressive woman who believed in the social reforms carried out under the revolutionary aegis. The Catholic values of charity and compassion, again not unrelated to female upper-class social sensitivity, were another source of Elena's vocation. These values were transmitted to her by the French nuns of the exclusive school in Mexico City where she was educated. The nuns encouraged students to visit the poor and to offer them food and other assistance. An additional source of inspiration for Elena was the radical social reformism and nationalism of her paternal uncle, who was an advisor to president Lázaro Cárdenas (1934–1940). Thus, her vocation came from a mixture of gender and class expectations, religious beliefs, and secular revolutionary nationalism, ideologies that may appear contradictory but that have been historically compatible for the Mexican upper classes (Adler Lomnitz and Pérez Lizaur 1987; Gledhill 2002).

Adler Lomnitz and Pérez Lizaur argue that the Mexican upper class combines the Catholic tradition with an anticlericalism that originated in nineteenth-century liberal ideas and that became radicalized with the influence of Marxism after the 1910 Revolution. A gender division of labor helps to reconcile these opposed traditions: women are closer to Catholic sensitivity, whereas men tend to present themselves as anticlerical. Religiousness and anticlericalism are constructed respectively as female and male domains. However, Elena's position in relation to the Church and religion was ambivalent. She criticized the Salesian priests with whom we collaborated in the neighborhood, because she found them irrational and ignorant. The rivalry between Elena's community development program and the Salesian fathers' program also triggered her antipathy. In addition, Elena despised poor people's religiosity, which she found superstitious and irrational. However, she acknowledged that the Church carried out important social work. Elena explained to me that the Church's social assistance programs tend to be cheaper and more efficient than those of the state because the Church counts on highly committed personnel who work not for money but for spiritual satisfaction.

In her career as a social worker, Elena demonstrated great commitment to improving the lot of the underprivileged. She decided to develop her social sensitivity in a professional way and earned a degree in social work. Highlighting her spirit of self-sacrifice, she claimed that her family and friends did not understand or support her choice of career. In Mexico City, she supervised religious nonprofit organizations for the state. Later, in the United States, she worked at a Mexican consulate, defending with passion vulnerable migrants, particularly children. In our community development program, she crossed the border daily and worked long hours to help the indigenous migrant community. If needed, she would fight with the Mexican police to rescue minors detained for illegal street vending and return them to their mothers.

Her commitment did not mean that she envisioned an egalitarian society, however. The director stated in informal conversations that the poor were profoundly different socially, psychologically, morally, and even physically from people like her. She argued, for example, that poor indigenous women do not need hospitals to give birth as much as "we" do because their bodies, perhaps, are less sensitive to pain. She also thought that indigenous culture was essentially different. According to her, a proof of cultural differences was that indigenous women never looked into "your" eyes and never expressed their opinions and desires. Elena constructed the result of centuries of oppression, in which indigenous women had to hide their subjectivity, as part of their culture. Elena also believed that the poor were largely responsible for their own situation because they were ignorant, undisciplined, and irrational. Her understanding was not unlike the culture of poverty paradigm that held the poor responsible for their own lot. Her perception also resembled a Latin American tradition of social work that assumed "that the poor were poor because they were unhygienic, dirty, ignorant and hereditarily unfit" (Stepan 1991, 37). Elena believed that, with proper training in discipline, hygiene, and moral values, the poor could become good employees and could enjoy a decent standard of living. In fact, she perceived this as her own nationalist agenda. She did not believe, however, that mobility into the middle class was appropriate for them. For instance, she did not consider that the poor or their children would be able to profit from higher education. Neither did she envision them as independent entrepreneurs. She thought that it was more appropriate for them to learn to follow directions and become reliable workers.

To sum up, Elena's worldview was complex; she was committed to social work and she challenged her husband and friends, who teased her and did not take her work seriously. She understood herself as a progressive woman, rational, independent, critical of PRI, which was then the ruling party; she was a supporter of the radical PRD, sympathetic to the rights of indigenous people and to the need for indigenous autonomy in the context of the Chiapas uprising. However, she was conscious of social differences and believed it would not be possible or desirable to overcome them.

The upbringing and worldview of the rest of the team varied. When the program started, the psychologist, Rosa, specialized in development aspects related to health care and hygiene. She made contact with a medical student and brought him to the neighborhood twice a week to vaccinate and check the health of children, and she taught indigenous women birth control methods and hygienic practices to raise their children such as ways to avoid and treat diarrhea and to avoid the spread of disease. Hygiene, health, and birth control were important parts of the program when it started, but these activities became less salient with time, particularly when Rosa left the program for another job. Eventually, the program focused more and more on its most bureaucratic aspects. Even before she left, Rosa ended up performing increasingly and then exclusively bureaucratic tasks.

Xoxitl, the lawyer, was a young woman who had been born in Tijuana into a migrant family of modest means from Michoacan. She had just completed her degree in law at the local public university and was hired because she knew Tijuana's society well and had good contacts with the police and the bureaucracy. Her job was to interview immigrants with the goal of gathering information about human rights violations by the Mexican police or the U.S. Border Patrol. She was also expected to advise migrants in legal matters and refer them to nongovernmental organizations that provided food and shelter for those in need. Her treatment of immigrants reflected the same attitude as Elena's, but Xoxitl was less compassionate and more distant. She emphasized her newly acquired status as a lawyer, referring to mature immigrant men as "young man" (*joven*) and giving them orders. She interviewed men who were waiting to cross the border and asked them why they were crossing illegally, then suggested that they return to their towns in the south of Mexico and apply for a legal visa. Immigrants laughed at her suggestion. While she was interviewing at the border, she emphasized the need to distinguish migrants (*migrantes*) from criminals (*maleantes*). According to her, both groups were very similar, but it was possible to differentiate them if "we" paid attention to some details: Migrants, for example, did not have keys in their pockets because they had left everything behind, whereas criminals had keys because they lived in Tijuana. Criminals often had a comb in their pockets and were neatly groomed, whereas immigrants looked as if they had not taken a shower or combed their hair in several days. Unlike Rosa, who left the program in frustration, Xoxitl was promoted to a better position at the research center.

One of the students was from Tijuana. She was completing her degree at the public university and was doing her community work with us. She did have a commitment to the education of indigenous migrants and worked hard at her job. She disagreed with Elena's methods and tried to persuade her to change them so that they would become more effective. Elena did not listen to her, and, like Rosa, this student eventually became frustrated.

Unlike Elena, who enjoyed working with poor and marginal people, the other team members, with the exception of a couple of students, understood their work as only a job for which they were paid or for which they got credit. They tried to avoid physical contact with "marginal" people. For Elena, contact with the poor was not problematic; it was desirable because it legitimized her as a compassionate member of the upper class. The fear and disgust that the middle- and lower-middle-class women felt in relation to the "marginals" can be explained as anxiety about their own social status. According to Mary Jackman (1994), dominant groups choose spatial segregation from subordinate groups when they are anxious about their status. When power relations are stable and well defined, dominant groups do not need to avoid intimate contact with subordinates.

Our development team functioned in an authoritarian manner. The director alone designed all our goals and strategies. She expected the rest of the team to show deference by letting her pick the best seat, serving her coffee, and handing her things. Although she asked for advice occasionally, she decided even on the most trivial matters and was not open to criticism. The rest of the team, limited to complying with her desires or to resisting silently, eventually became frustrated.

The Trip to the Community: The Discourse of Difference

Elena always determined conversation topics. She began and ended conversations, and the rest of us limited ourselves to making brief remarks on the topics of her choice. There were some recurrent conversation pieces, and they always tended to mark social differences, either among the members of the group when we traveled toward the community, or between the group as a whole and the "marginal" population when we returned. When we went to the community, the director often chose topics that revealed her social class. She spoke about her travels to Europe and within the United States, and about art and literature. Elena often complained because a cosmopolitan and refined woman like herself was forced to live and work between such a provincial region of her country and, even worse, in the other side of the border. As a Mexican nationalist, she often expressed contempt for the United States. Some of her monologues were based on a comparison between Mexico City and the northern region of Mexico, in which the north was constructed as provincial and unsophisticated and Mexico City as cosmopolitan and refined. Most women in the team, with the exception of the upper-class student and me, were from the north of Mexico, and they seemed to feel uncomfortable with Elena's remarks. The conversation occasionally centered on events that had involved Elena's family or friends. She spoke about her husband's taste for golf, about his businesses, and about her children's studies in elite universities in the United States, subjects that emphasized the differences between the director and the rest of the team. However, Elena also criticized her own social class. She told us, for example, that one of her friends had decided to gather the domestic workers of all her other friends to instruct them in moral issues, which Elena thought was a stupid idea. Elena also questioned her husband's opinions and constructed him as conservative and socially insensitive. However, her complaints did not reflect an important ideological difference with her partner; she assumed that women are more sensitive than men, and she defined her husband's lack of social sensitivity as part of his masculinity. She often compared her husband's conservative ideas (which she also perceived as realistic) to those of her children, who supported indigenous rights and progressive social movements. The role of the father was to be a "realist," because he was in charge of increasing the family's wealth, whereas women and children could afford to be sensitive without endangering their class privileges.

When we returned from the community, the most common conversation topic was a reflection on the nature of the poor, the marginal, and the Indian. This reflection took place in the context of the difficulties that we encountered when we tried to work with the community and the rejection that we experienced from community members. The conversations about "marginals" or Indians explored what the social workers understood as the profound differences between these people and "people like us." Our difficulties were caused, according to the social workers, by the "marginals" or the Indians who were too ignorant or too poor to understand our work and sacrifice. Elena argued that we knew what was good for community people but that it was not easy to transmit our knowledge to them, or to get them to collaborate. As in any paternalist relationship, we assumed our intellectual and moral superiority over "the poor" (Jackman 1994; Van der Veer 1986). Elena's excuses for the failures of the program were also addressed to me. She considered Europeans and North Americans naive because they do not take into account existing social and ethnic differences that cannot be easily overcome.

The development team did not practice self-criticism. When I started to collaborate with the program, the first task that Elena assigned to me was to find out why the community did not cooperate with her. She thought that the lack of cooperation was due to some kind of rivalry or feud between Mixtec groups arriving from different towns. When I investigated the matter, I found that the lack of cooperation was due to Elena's authoritarian style and, more important, the perception that the program was not providing benefits to the community. Mixtec women complained that the program was not giving them a steady job or a real opportunity to educate themselves. When I delicately suggested some of these issues to the director, she was offended. She said that Indians were unable to appreciate or understand the work we were doing for them. Critical scholars argue that it is common for NGOs to blame their target populations for the failure of their development efforts, instead of reflecting on what went wrong with their own strategies (Delpino and Pasara 1991).

In their daily conversations, social workers shifted from the idea that the culture of "marginals" was the cause of their sad situation to more essentialist constructions of difference and inferiority. Elena argued that "marginals" were characterized by irrational attitudes. For that reason, they were easy prey of religious groups and sects that hindered their progress. She also doubted the intellectual ability of Indians. The informal discourse of social workers associated being Indian with poverty, ignorance, and irrationality; sometimes, especially among the college students, who tended to be more idealistic, that construction was combined with a more romantic representation of Indians as traditional, harmonious, and exotic. This second construction surfaced, for example, when Indians were asked to do collective work for the program, or to celebrate their patron saint in their region's style. However, both understandings emphasized differences between Indians and the rest of the population. The social workers' conversations were ambivalent in relation to the cause, nature, and scope of social and ethnic differences. Were cultural differences the result of centuries of impoverishment and exploitation? Was a defective culture what kept Indians in poverty and ignorance and hindered their progress? Were differences essential and almost biological? The biological roots of inferiority were often suggested but were never openly defended because biological racism is not considered politically correct in Mexico.

Grassroots Participation, Authoritarianism,
and the Limits of Development

The research center spent few resources directly on the Mixtec community. It invested very little on working space, technology, educational, and other materials and used mostly what was already available in the neighborhood. For example, the program borrowed space and tools from the Salesian priests and educational materials from the National Institute for Adult Education. Elena spoke with the Salesian fathers, who let her use their community center in Valle Verde as labor space for the cooperative. According to Elena, the cooperative did not need a permanent building, only a center where organizers and workers could meet periodically. Elena expected the women to work at home. She explained the advantages of home labor to me: it lowers infrastructure and production costs; it reduces the responsibility of the firm for its employees; and the employer can count on the (unpaid) collaboration of the whole family. When the relationships with the Salesians deteriorated as a result of rivalry between both programs after the Salesians got a major grant for the government, our program started to use the neighborhood's public school. The program's only significant investment in the community were a few grants that the research center gave to the indigenous elementary school for particular projects, such as the construction of an extra room for multiple uses. However, the research center was able to pay middle-class salaries to a few professionals and buy a jeep for the exclusive use of the development team. The community development program also had elegant offices located at the research center. This was a case in which the overhead expenses seemed bigger than the actual investment in the community, a key problem of NGO–led development that has been identified by Arellano and Petras (1994) and other authors.

In contrast to what the research center's promotional materials stated, the program of direct assistance and the cooperative were neither participatory nor democratic. The cooperative's foundational documents established that indigenous migrants were its owners and that they would manage the firm democratically through an assembly and elected representatives. In practice, Elena made most decisions and then gathered the necessary signatures from community members, who signed without even reading the paperwork. Indigenous migrants did not identify the cooperative as their own and perceived Elena as a *patrona*, or an occasional employer.

As soon as the cooperative was publicized in the United States business community by marketing consultants hired by Elena and Mexican state institutions in charge of United States–Mexico economic relations (which Elena knew well through her husband), a few firms became interested in the cheap labor it offered. For example, the Mexican Bank of Exterior Commerce found two North American employers that were interested in "the group of Mixtec families that offer services of cheap labor." One was a floral design company and the other a company that made seasonal arrangements for large retailers, such as Target and Kmart. However, Elena did not sign contracts with the two contracting firms because she considered the wages they proposed too low. According to a study done by a student who was completing his M.A. at the research center, indigenous women were able to make between $8 U.S. and $10 U.S. in a good day in the informal economy, meeting and even exceeding the average industrial wage in the area, which was, at the time, $8 U.S. per day. These two firms wanted to pay these women a wage below the local average because indigenous migrants lacked the cultural resources of urban mestizo workers. Finally, the cooperative (read Elena) accepted a contract with a Korean firm that assembled components of TVs and VCRs for Sony. Indigenous women were paid piecework. According to our director, women workers should be able to assemble 800 pieces a day and make a salary of up to $8 U.S. (still less than what, according to the study, they would be able to make in the informal economy). However, indigenous women complained that they were only able to assemble around 200 pieces and, thus, to make only $2 U.S. per day. Not surprisingly, none of the women left the informal economy to pursue this opportunity. Those who could afford to left informal activities for fear of police harassment, and others preferred to combine work in the cooperative during the week with informal work selling crafts on the weekends when more tourists visited the city. A few women told me that they were working with the cooperative because they did not have anything better to do for the time being. However, in the documents exchanged between the program and prospective employers, businessmen subcontracting indigenous women for wages below the market were assumed to be doing charity and a good deed.

While waiting for industrial contracts, the cooperative produced some textile crafts for local and international consumption under the leadership of our program. Although our flyers advertised indigenous migrants' dexterity and craftsmanship, our director believed that indigenous women would not be able to produce quality Mexican crafts. According to her, Mexican crafts were the result of a long, sophisticated tradition. Some indigenous groups, such as the Zapotecs, did have a history of producing quality crafts, but, according to Elena, this was not the case of the Mixtecs, who were mostly subsistence peasants. Elena explained that the Mixtecs produced a few crafts, such as palm-leaf hats in their region of origin, but there was no palm available in Tijuana with which they could work. Elena believed that indigenous women would do better copying designs from North American magazines that reflected a more simple and unsophisticated culture that indigenous women, with their allegedly limited capabilities, would be able to grasp better. Our director's articulation of nationalism and anti-Americanism with racial prejudices was peculiar, because crafts have been historically associated with indigenous peoples in post-Revolutionary Mexico (Dietz 1995). Elena's doubts about the intellectual capacity of indigenous women and their ability to learn were one of the main obstacles for the success of our efforts. I tried to convince Elena that we should focus on selling the ethnicity of Mixtec women to progressive consumers in the United States and perhaps Europe. These consumers would appreciate the social content of the product. However, Elena did not consider ethnicity something that could be sold, because she did not think that ethnicity had an intrinsic value that could attract people. She kept thinking about indigenous migrant women as a cheap labor force that could be used to manufacture some simple product that did not require refined skills and intellectual capacity. Despite Elena's fears, the textiles produced by the cooperative were well received by the local public, particularly because of the cooperative's social orientation. Two European foundations and a Mexican government institution dedicated to the promotion of popular cultures became interested in helping finance our operations. Our director declined their offers. She argued that indigenous women were better suited for industrial than creative craftwork. In addition, perhaps Elena wished to avoid the interference of other institutions in our program and to prevent others from taking credit for what we were doing. A group of indigenous women were able to make approximately $30 U.S. a month each with the sale of textiles in the local market. In the Mexican border region, this meant that they received an extra income, but not a living wage, during this period.

Elena also signed a contract with an elegant golf resort and real estate development located in the Baja California coast. Mixtec women produced bags in which to store golf balls and other golf accessories. In addition, the resort sponsored a concert for the benefit of the research center's human rights program. The representative of the resort told me that she thought that the good publicity achieved by helping the research center and the indigenous community would help her market the resort as a cultural center to North Americans, who were the majority of her customers. Our program got enough money from this concert to build the extra room for the bilingual school in Valle Verde. On another occasion, Elena asked Mixtec women to produce Jewish decorations for a religious shop on the other side of the border. In both cases, Mixtec women copied designs that represented things and worlds they did not understand. The meaning of what they were doing was not explained to them.

In our reading and writing classes, the teaching style was also authoritarian. Indigenous women were asked to copy, recite, or memorize without emphasis on comprehension. This was very problematic, especially because these women spoke Mixtec as their first language and were not completely fluent in Spanish. Our director explained to us how to teach: "It is not necessary for them to understand what they are reading. They are not going to understand. You have to tell them exactly what to do. They should learn to follow directions. Perhaps they will understand eventually. But if they never understand, this training will at least be useful for them." Again, our director demonstrated a profound lack of confidence in indigenous women's abilities beyond following directions and simple manual work.

There was very little communication between our students and us. Mixtec women, for their part, tried to learn reading and writing while reducing their communication with social workers to a minimum. The program was not training indigenous women for independence and self-sufficiency, as the president of the research center wished. On the contrary, it was attempting to train them in obedience and docility. I tried to do something different with the students assigned to me. I tried to communicate with them and teach them to read and write words that I assumed they were interested in learning, such as their children's names, street signs, and so on. I also tried to learn some words in their language as I taught them mine. My efforts, however, were not successful. When I tried to communicate with them so they would understand what they were reading or writing, they thought that I was wasting their time. They believed that what they should do to learn to read and write was to fill in, consecutively, the pages of the official book provided by the National Institute for Adult Education. They believed that this activity would allow them eventually to acquire their elementary school certificates. Perhaps this attitude revealed an insight on the part of these women into the nature of literacy: literacy for them may have meant an official qualification that would open better job opportunities for them. From this point of view, their understanding of literacy, unlike mine, was quite practical. Was my own less-practical understanding of literacy a class and ethnic privilege?

When I suggested to Elena that the women were not learning, and that, perhaps, we should rethink our methodology, she answered that the problem was that the women were not interested in learning. According to Elena, they were so poor and ignorant that they did not understand the importance of literacy because they had more pressing needs. However, I had observed Mixtec women stubbornly trying to learn so that they could get their certificates, until they realized that it was impossible and gave up.

Although literacy classes were not as successful as they should have been, they soon became an official institution. The program had an agreement with the National Institute for Adult Education (INEA) to prepare students for the official exams. Once a month, we received the visit of a coordinator from the Institute, who inspected our classes and administered the exams. Our program was one of the few providers of adult education in the neighborhood, but the program's social workers lacked the skills, and in some cases the commitment, to be successful in their task.

Although the INEA coordinator was aware of our program's shortcomings, he continued to collaborate with it. INEA receives few state resources and must work almost entirely with volunteers.

Like other activities, the medical attention provided by the program was not very efficient. A medical student went to the neighborhood once every fifteen days to vaccinate children and examine them. This student did not have a strong commitment to the community. He spent the morning talking to his nurse or hanging out in the Salesian center's doorway. If someone brought a sick child to him, he examined him or her without enthusiasm, trying to avoid physical contact with the child as much as he could. Despite the medical student's negative attitude, the vaccination campaigns were useful for neighborhood's children. Elena also got medical attention for some neighborhood residents who needed it badly. She went out of her way to help the indigenous and the poor in this manner.

The most successful aspect of the program was the processing of birth certificates for Mixtec children and adults. We collaborated with governmental institutions, such as the National Indigenist Institute and the Tijuana Civil Registry, because the state was interested in building a record of this very mobile population, and the National Indigenist Institute had created a special program for the registration of indigenous migrants (INI-SEDESOL 1994). In addition, Mixtec migrants needed these documents to prove that they were Mexicans and to have access to their citizenship rights to education, health, and so on.

Some mestizos also asked us for help in getting their documents, but the program could not help them. We could only provide documents for Indians through the National Indigenist Institute. Indians were believed to need help because they were not fluent in Spanish, they had a low level of formal education, and they were vulnerable to discrimination. Because of the special status enjoyed by Indians and the idea that they needed protection, both the program and the National Indigenist Institute could mediate for them as a group. Mestizos, on the contrary, had to establish a personalized relationship with the state. This led to resentment on the part of mestizos, who sometimes claimed to be Indians from this or that ethnic group in order to receive help. The special status that the program gave to Indians helped magnify existing envies and enmities between neighbors. Mixtecs appeared to be interested in our bureaucratic services and grateful for them. We spared them the mistreatment and discrimination they would have suffered in government offices, and sometimes we accompanied them to government offices. Because they were our clients and were protected by us, they received special treatment. They did not receive this treatment because they had rights as Mexican citizens but because they were clients of our program and the research center was influential in Tijuana. It is important to note that Elena struggled to deliver their rights to indigenous people and vigorously challenged any kind of mistreatment by other government officials.

To sum up, the project fell short of its stated goals; it did not provide steady jobs for indigenous women in their own community so they would be able to leave the informal economy and it did not educate them to become independent, self-sufficient citizens. Even our director's goal of training them in urban industrial discipline was achieved only superficially because indigenous women progressively abandoned the program when they figured out that they would find neither good jobs, useful learning opportunities, nor adequate health care through us. In addition, border employers were not convinced that this was a reliable labor force that they could use. However, the program carried out an important work for the state, helping to regularize and control a mobile, marginal population. As Ferguson (1990) notes, development programs often fail in their own terms, but they are successful most of the time in expanding the reach of the state over marginal regions and populations.

Daily Interactions, Social Cohesion, and the Reproduction of Social and Ethnic Differences

Mary Jackman (1994) argues that the energies of dominant groups concentrate not on exercising power by force but rather on persuading the dominated and preventing conflict. The use of force is not an expression of power but an expression of the failure of power, the failure to obtain the complicity and the obedience of the subordinate Other. Dominant groups make efforts to teach the subordinate a common worldview that rationalizes the existing order. The upper and middle classes use charity and, in this case, community development, to enter into contact with the poor and the nonwhite, to teach them that the privileged are benign and care about them, and to try to shape the subalterns in the image that the privileged have of them. Jackman argues that physical contact between social groups does not take place in a neutral framework but rather in a context that allows the dominant group a natural advantage in any encounter. Dominant groups feel the need to differentiate themselves from the subordinate through everyday behaviors that reinforce their class and ethnic prerogatives. According to Jackman, these behaviors include tone of voice and way of addressing people, invasions of personal space, and how conversations begin and end.

Elena's aim was to re-create in her development work a personalized, maternalist relationship with people in the neighborhood. She showed that she sincerely cared for community members while marking the differences between her and them through a number of behaviors similar to those described by Jackman. Elena learned people's names and details about their lives, she often asked them how they were doing, and she tried to help as much as she could. In exchange, she expected deference and loyalty. Sometimes, community members responded positively to her attempts. In other cases, they resisted the ties of love and domination that she tried to impose on them. For instance, not all indigenous migrants came near us when Elena called them; some pretended not to see or hear us and continued walking. Most young men tried to avoid us, whereas elderly men and women of all ages were more open to interaction with us. One explanation for this behavior could be that indigenous men felt emasculated when Elena talked to them as if they were little children, as she often did with Indians and the poor. For example, one of the indigenous teachers in the neighborhood, whom Elena treated like a child, referred to us as "the little ladies" (*las damitas*), in an attempt to transgress power relations and perhaps to recover some of his hurt masculinity. Another possibility is that young men avoided us because they did not need us. Most of them had jobs, while it was more difficult for the elderly and women with children to find jobs. Even women and elderly men ignored us if they did not need our help. They only submitted to the maternalist treatment of our program when they thought they needed us.

One of the ways the program's maternalism and authoritarianism manifested itself in everyday interactions was through the treatment of Indians as children. Elena often talked to Indians with the mellow tone adults use when they talk to children. To deprive the Other of his or her adulthood and to assume a motherly role is a way to disempower the Other, because age is a source of status in most societies.

Elena tried to control both the spaces and the bodies of indigenous people. When we took a walk in the neighborhood, we typically visited some houses. Elena knocked on the door loudly and commanded the woman or man inside to come out and receive us. She neither made appointments nor asked the neighbors whether they would like to be visited. Indigenous people came out of their houses with a face that showed either shyness or distrust, and Elena commanded them to invite us in. For her, the "marginals" did not have the right to privacy. Elena also felt entitled to control their sexuality. She asked indigenous women how many children they had. They looked toward the floor shyly, and answered that they had seven or eight children. "Eight children," Elena said. "We will have to tie your legs up."

The concepts of cleanliness and dirt were another way to regulate social interactions and reinforce ethnic and class differences. Mary Douglas (1966) notes that in most societies forms of impurity are used as analogies to express a general vision of the social order. Subordinate groups are often constructed as dirty and impure. In the case of our program, the idea that indigenous migrants and their surroundings were dirty helped to maintain ethnic differences and to separate the spaces occupied by different groups.

Paradoxically, Elena wished to control and invade the Mixtecs' spaces and persons while keeping them physically separate from us. When I began to work in the program, social workers informed me that we could neither eat nor go to the bathroom in the community. We should eat and urinate before leaving for the neighborhood. We did not introduce into our bodies anything that came from the neighborhood. By arriving in the community as people without physical needs, we perhaps reinforced our symbolic power and underscored social differences. On the other hand, this behavior had a material basis, as the hygienic conditions of a neighborhood without running water and drainage were not the best.

We were often invited to eat in the community, but the social workers never drank or ate what was offered to them unless it was an industrial product, such as a bottle of soda that was considered clean. The director explained herself with us. We should not think that she did not want to eat with Indians, but she could not control her repugnance because her mother had taught her since she was a child that she should not eat anything in the street. As anthropologists know very well, to eat with somebody is a way to share, to acknowledge equality, and to have access to the other person's world. To reject indigenous migrants' food was a way to demonstrate inequality and separation. Pierre Bourdieu's (1977) concept of habitus helps explain this kind of behavior. The actions of social workers did not reflect a conscious desire to maintain social and ethnic differences; rather, they were the product of the education that members of a certain social class had received since childhood and as such were practiced almost unconsciously.

It is worth noting that the social workers felt as much repugnance for indigenous food as indigenous people felt interest in having us eating with them, even though they were people of modest means for whom food, especially meat, was very expensive. Indigenous people's interest in eating with us perhaps reflected a desire to blur social differences and to demonstrate equality, or perhaps it was a way to please us and create durable links with us.

Indigenous migrants had internalized the idea of their own dirt. They often felt ashamed to share spaces with people from a different social class. On one occasion, we were driving an indigenous family to city hall to run some errands. Before entering the car, they cleaned their shoes for about twenty minutes. Finally, they decided to take them off before entering the car. Once inside, they shrank to occupy as little space as possible. Needless to say, none of the social workers wanted to share the space in the back of the car with them. On another occasion, an indigenous teacher was driving me to the city. He told me that he felt ashamed that I entered his car, because it was dirty and smelled bad.

The attempts of indigenous migrants to be clean, and thus to show us that they were "civilized," were never enough for the social workers, who seemed not to appreciate them. For example, we were invited to have lunch in an indigenous house to celebrate a wedding. The hostess had reserved the best table for us, and we were expected to eat alone, while indigenous women served us. They ate at another table out of our sight, perhaps because they felt ashamed or uncomfortable to eat with us, perhaps, because they thought that we would not like to sit next to them, or perhaps to show deference to us. Before eating, the hostess asked us to wash our hands. She had a receptacle containing clean water to wash our hands and provided clean paper towels to dry them. She was making an effort to show us how clean she was, that she had learned her lesson. However, Elena reprimanded her because the soap was too coarse. The hostess felt ashamed and humiliated. Her effort had been considerable: her house lacked running water, and paper towels are expensive luxury items in the neighborhood.

The faces of the social workers when the food arrived reflected the repugnance that they felt. Elena told the Mixtec woman that she would not eat meat. When the woman asked why, Elena answered laughing that her religion forbade her to eat meat. Not only was she showing strong distaste for the food, but she was mocking what she thought were the irrational beliefs of "marginals." As each of the dishes containing rice and chicken mole arrived, the social workers passed them from one to another, repugnance showing in their faces, until there was no one else without a plate. They ate the mole with disgust, ignoring the fact that it is considered an expensive delicacy by the Mixtecs.

Conclusion

Did the nongovernmental organization that I observed promote development and class and ethnic democratization on the Mexican side of the border, or did it reinforce existing power relations, including an authoritarian and discriminatory culture? I believe there is no simple answer to these questions. The answer depends in part on the point of view adopted by the observer and on what he or she envisions as development and democratization. Our director's goal to transform a group of immigrant women of peasant origin into a disciplined industrial labor force available to national and transnational capitalists can be judged as an effort to reproduce the historical subordination of indigenous women or, perhaps, to transform this subordination to fit the changing needs of national and international bourgeoisies. At the Mexican border, it is believed that industrial jobs are beyond the abilities of indigenous migrant women, however. Wages in the industrial sector are typically double those in the agricultural sector. In the mid-1990s, a maquiladora worker made around $8 U.S. a day, whereas an agricultural day laborer in neighboring export-oriented fields made around $4 U.S. In this context, Elena was perceived as a visionary who wanted to move indigenous women one step further by opening better-paid and higher-status opportunities for them. Moreover, in the context of traditional post-Revolutionary Mexican interpretations of ethnicity, as soon as these women learned Spanish, mastered reading and writing skills, and joined the urban economy, they would be regarded as mestizas, which in Mexico has historically meant an improvement in social status. However, our program did not consciously aim to assimilate indigenous migrants into the masses of urban mestizos. On the contrary, we celebrated what the director understood as indigenous culture; paradoxically, these were folk Catholic celebrations. In addition, the facts that our program specifically and exclusively addressed indigenous migrants and that indigenous and mestizo neighbors were treated differently reinforced ethnic rivalries in the neighborhood. Moreover, the prejudices felt and expressed by social workers did not facilitate the integration of indigenous people to mestizo Mexico. In this chapter, the term "indigenous migrant" has been used almost interchangeably with "poor" and "marginal." Both the director of the research center and the director of the program perceived indigenous migrants as representing an extreme case of poverty—"the poorest among the poor." As we have seen, other constructions of ethnicity surfaced on occasion, but this was the dominant one.

Our program fell short of even reaching Elena's goals, however limited, utilitarian, or even morally wrong they may appear to have been. The reason for this failure was community resistance: indigenous women slowly stopped attending the program when they realized it would not bring them a steady, decently paying job or real learning opportunities. Indigenous women could not get the job they wanted partly because they had to compete with more seasoned urban workers. In addition, the possibility of profiting from a relatively rewarding informal economy fueled by international tourism provided indigenous women an alternative to industrial work. From another perspective, the failure of the cooperative and the literacy campaign resulted from the lack of confidence Elena and other staff members had in the learning ability of these women. These prejudices precluded our program from undertaking more creative strategies for the cooperative and for teaching reading and writing.

The bureaucratic functions that our development program performed could also be interpreted in two ways. On the one hand, we were extending the reach of the state over this mobile marginal population (Ferguson 1990). On the other hand, we were helping these migrants gain access to their citizenship rights, however limited, and to a formal job, social security, education, and public health by assisting them in obtaining official identity documents. By being able to demonstrate that they were Mexican citizens, as opposed to Central American or South American immigrants on their way to the United States, indigenous migrants would be able to avoid police and military harassment (interviews conducted by author with INI government officials).

The collective civil weddings that we organized could also have two readings. They could be interpreted as an attempt to moralize this population according to bourgeois and middle-class standards. Our director, however, affirmed, not without reason, that civil marriage would protect indigenous women's rights to family property and economic support from their partners.

There were clear limits to the amount of democratization for which our program was able to aim, and I argue that these limits were linked to the class and ethnic background of development workers. Elena believed that, with some effort on our part and their part, indigenous migrants could become good proletarians; she neither envisioned nor desired their mobility, or their children's mobility, into the middle class. Adler Lomnitz and Pérez Lizaur (1987) have argued that the Mexican upper class is not characterized by racist prejudices, although they show preference for blond, blue-eyed people. A detailed study of Elena's worldview, discourse, and practices as she worked with indigenous migrants shows that she had deeply engrained prejudices that can be interpreted as part of her education as a member of the upper class. Elena thought that indigenous migrants could learn to follow but not to lead. She interpreted the results of domination as cultural difference (as when she argued that not looking into the eyes or not expressing their needs and desires was part of indigenous culture). Finally, Elena even suggested on occasion the possibility of innate physical differences. She never defended this position aggressively, however, because biological racism is not politically correct in Mexico.

Other members of the team discriminated against indigenous

migrants somewhat differently. They did not seem to have deeply engrained beliefs about other people's inferiority, and, unlike Elena, they were worried about marking the boundaries between the Indian, the marginal, and themselves. In other words, they were constructing the boundaries instead of taking them for granted. Their new, upwardly mobile identity and their desire to maintain it shaped their discriminatory treatment of others.

However, all this discrimination took place in a framework in which social workers sincerely believed themselves to be working for the community's good. A discussion of paternalism, and in this case maternalism, becomes necessary here. Social workers felt that they were morally superior to indigenous migrants at the same time that they were convinced that they were acting on the community's behalf. To reinforce the maternal link, they treated community members like children, depriving them of the symbolic power that comes with age. Elena attempted to impose her own idea of the good on capable adults who, perhaps, had different aims and interests. The main problem was that Elena's idea of the good included the preservation of marked social hierarchies. Indigenous migrants often resisted the maternalism of Elena and other staff members, and they only accepted it when they were expecting tangible benefits from us.

The liberal philosopher Donald Van der Veer (1986) defines paternalism as interference with the autonomy of another person for that person's good. He argues that paternalism can be justified only when the recipient of paternalism is incompetent, as in the case of children or mentally handicapped people. Otherwise, paternalism is not justified, because it means constructing the other person as inferior and interfering with that person's autonomy and idea of the good. Van der Veer notes that a recurrent problem in the history of liberalism has been the treatment of the poor, racial and ethnic minorities, and women as incompetent. He calls this kind of paternalism "aggressive benevolence." It could be argued that our program was practicing this kind of strong paternalism, which, according to Van der Veer, is not justified, because it is based on lack of respect for the other.

The class background and habitus of development workers limited the kinds of social changes that we could aim for as an institution, but the experience cannot be condemned altogether. Seen from the local context, the program worked toward the social mobility, however limited, of indigenous women. Is the case discussed here representative of NGO–led development, or is it an exception that can be explained by the individual personality of the director? Even if this is a unique case, we can learn a few things from it. First, I argue, along with other critical scholars of development and NGOs, that the researcher should not take at face value the discourse of these organizations, and should investigate their practices as well as the effects of these practices for affected populations. Second, the people who have access to the know-how and resources to create nongovernmental organizations in non-Western societies are often members of the upper and middle classes. These development workers cannot be placed outside the particular histories and fields of force of their own societies. As Abramson (1999) has noted, it is a mistake to expect grassroots development to work from outside a particular society.

Conclusion

Cultural Difference and Democracy

This book is a reflection on the creation and meaning of differences and identities in contexts that not only take into account those whose identity is being discussed, in this case indigenous migrants, but also more powerful actors like the state, capital, elites, and intellectuals. My interest has been not to reify these actors but to present them as individuals and groups in their complexity and sometimes ambivalence, a project for which the ethnographic method is ideal. It has been my intention to place them in the context of particular political-economic local and global processes and social relations. To achieve this, I have combined the ethnographic method with the discussion of secondary literature, the press, unpublished documents, and archival sources.

A central component of the book has been the discussion of who is emphasizing difference for whom and, more specifically, the consequences of emphasizing differences that are constructed over an inequality that they tend to reproduce for a democratic society. It is important to clarify at this point that this book is not a manifesto against difference in and of itself. In Latin America in the future I would like to see more and better bilingual-bicultural schools (Martínez Novo 2004); more diverse mainstream schools that teach respect for real others rather than teaching stereotypes; a revitalization of indigenous languages when indigenous people so desire; and indigenous people (as well as people of African descent, women, and other marginalized groups) presenting themselves as they wish in the media, academia, all kinds of rewarding jobs, politics, and so on. I feel that tolerance, recognition of difference, and respect for the choices of others, as long as these choices do not endanger the liberty and physical or psychological integrity of other individuals,[1] are essential to the construction of radical democracy.[2] However, as Nancy Fraser (1996) has so persuasively argued, radical democracy should be built not only on recognition but also on redistribution of economic and other resources. This second task is even more urgent in Latin America, one of the most unequal areas of the world. Fraser urges us to rethink which differences are the result of inequality and should be eliminated and which differences are positive for a diverse and tolerant society and should be protected and cherished. In other words, according to Fraser, and I strongly agree with her, not all differences are the same and not all differences are worth preserving. What worries me in the case of indigenous migrants in Baja California is the imposition from above of a selected understanding of difference—one that tends to construct the results of inequality as culture or tradition—and the disguise of this imposed concept of culture as a grassroots creation or choice.

Throughout the book, I have argued that difference at the Mexican border often implies hierarchy. The "indigenous migrant" label is associated with vulnerability and low socioeconomic status. In the San Quintín Valley, Indian status is linked to a particular form of harsh, low-paid temporary labor: indigenous migrants are preferred day laborers in commercial agriculture, and day laborers are defined as indigenous, whether or not they speak an indigenous language and self-identify as Indian. Indian status, then, is associated with frugality, docility, and willingness to accept lower wages and harsher living conditions. In chapter 3, I refer to a government official who associates being Indian with poverty and lack of formal education to the point that educated and comfortable individuals cannot be labeled Indian under her assumptions. In the same chapter, I introduce an indigenous schoolteacher who explains being Indian to his pupils as a "lack"—a lack of proficiency in Spanish and reading ability, replicating the situation found by Judith Friedlander (1975) among Nahuatl speakers in the 1970s, a period that anteceded the development of the continental movement for Indian rights. In the press and in scholarly debate about indigenous women street vendors, various manifestations of poverty, such as making a living as a street vendor, child labor, and self-construction of homes in dangerous urban spaces, are defined by advocates of these women as cultural choices or traditions. Similarly, the nongovernmental organization where I worked interprets ethnicity as a form of vulnerability. Indigenous migrants deserve to be helped because they are particularly vulnerable—using a slogan popular in Mexico in the 1990s, they are "the poorest among the poor." Elena, the director of the community development program, also links the lack of expression of subjectivity (looking down when addressed by a member of the dominant class) with a different culture. This particular effect of a long-term training in social inequality is common among other oppressed groups. For example, bell hooks (1993), in an interesting essay entitled "Images of Whiteness in the Black Imagination," explains that North American slaves were not allowed to look their superiors in the eye or to express their opinions, whereas they could always be looked at or talked to. The suppression of the subjectivity of the oppressed is an important objective of domination.

In other instances throughout this book, the idea of culture is used to exclude or to justify the exclusion of indigenous migrants from economic and symbolic resources. For example, indigenous people are assumed to prefer their own traditional medicine to access to Western hospitals and medical facilities, despite the fact that organized day laborers had been fighting for a hospital for years. Some advocates (government officials, intellectuals, activists) think that indigenous culture should be protected from the outside influences that come from formal education, contact with foreign tourists, and North American aid groups. This attitude is problematic for three reasons: First, this form of "protection" through segregation would exclude indigenous people from important societal resources. Second, a strategy to regulate their right to resources, punishing those who discriminated against them and avoiding structural racism, would not be implemented. Finally, segregation is not a strategy chosen by indigenous migrants themselves but by their advocates. I argue that this paternalistic idea of protection through segregation has a colonial origin in the *Repúblicas de Indios* through which the Spanish Crown sought to protect indigenous people from rapacious colonists while keeping ethnic boundaries clear and intact in order to tax and extract labor from this population (Wolf 1982).

Is indigenous migrant status also associated with nonhierarchical difference or positive traits at the Mexican border? In some instances it is: government officials from the National Indigenist Institute genuinely understand ethnic identity as an appropriate tool for effective social organization that would help liberate indigenous migrants from oppression by employers and the government itself. The radio station of the National Indigenist Institute promotes the idea of the "civilized Indian" who knows his or her rights as well as possessing a dignified understanding of the "indigenous migrant." An official from the Department of Public Education asserts that Indians are generous and collaborative by nature. However this last representation is double-edged, because it can be used to justify the extraction of unpaid or cheap labor from the indigenous community and can function, therefore, as another source of vulnerability.

All in all, I argue that the stigma attached to Indian status still prevails over positive understandings of ethnicity in Baja California, although this may change with multicultural policies and indigenous rights struggles in the future. This is not necessarily the case for other indigenous groups in Latin America. In some instances, a positive valuation of Indian identity may outweigh the stigma attached to the label. This may be so in the case of the Otavalo merchants studied by Kyle (2000) and Colloredo-Mansfeld (1999) or the Zapotecs studied by Stephen (1991, 1996). These successful craft entrepreneurs have been able to take advantage of a market niche for the exotic in Europe and the United States. Even in these optimistic cases, Colloredo-Mansfeld (1999) argues that stigmatization is still predominant due to the legacy of colonial oppression, that not all Otavalos have been able to profit from this opportunity, and that the possibility for expansion of an economy focused on the sale of exotic wares is not unlimited. Lila Abu-Lughod (1991) argues that most of the time an emphasis on cultural difference implies hierarchy because the discursive construction of culture takes place in a context of Western colonial and postcolonial domination over non-Western peoples who are constructed as "cultural" or different. In the case of indigenous migrants at the Mexican border, how differences are shaped reflects the historical and current subordination of Indians throughout Mexico and of indigenous migrants in the north.

In this book I have discussed at length the problem of who is promoting the reinforcement of differences over whom. Because of the stigma attached to the label "Indian," many grassroots migrants wish to assimilate into mestizo northern Mexico. Recognition of difference is therefore not a claim that originates in the majority of grassroots migrants. As Dombrowski (2001) effectively shows, those for whom culture is too costly are likely to be "against culture," whereas other community members better situated to benefit from a reinforcement of native culture may be supportive of it, although not without ambivalence, as we see in the case of indigenous teachers in Tijuana. Moreover, according to Dombrowski some people may react to the same socioeconomic crisis in different ways: some may be "against" and some "for" culture. Dombrowski (2001, 184) writes,

> Important social divisions exist within every group—divisions of class, age, gender, or ethnicity—and these divisions make culture or "local meaning" an issue for struggle, not something unconsciously accepted among those in a particular locality. . . . In the past, many ethnologists were able to justify a notion of shared culture by ignoring these divisions. . . . Culture, in this view, is something that can be lost, but seldom is it considered something that might be or must be made and remade if it is to exist at all. And perhaps more importantly, when such making and remaking is done at the expense of some more than of others.

Indigenous migrant leaders do important work for the preservation of ethnic boundaries. It should, however, be acknowledged that many of these leaders have been trained by and work for the state as public school teachers. Others are union leaders whose organizations have developed close ties to the state and who are rewarded when they follow official lines. Others benefit from international funding when they reinforce differences, an issue that I have not explored in depth in this book but that has been discussed in length elsewhere (Brysk 2000). Still others react against discrimination and marginalization, reinforcing their Indianness but not at the expense of access to education and economic opportunities.

An important point of this book is that the voices of the leaders should not be taken uncritically for the grassroots points of view, that the ties of indigenous leaders and their organizations to the state and other social powers and societal levels should be acknowledged, and that the connections between those who speak as leaders and constituencies should not be taken for granted. For example, in an otherwise excellent book entitled *Indigenous Movements and Their Critics*, Kay Warren (1998) assumes that the discourses and positions of pan-Maya activists represent the whole indigenous community in Guatemala; she does this without examining in detail either the location of these leaders in larger social fields or the struggles over the construction and meaning of culture within the indigenous community. In addition, Warren dismisses all critics of indigenous leaders and movements of the right and the left as prejudiced. They may very well be in the case she studies, but I am worried about the anthropological construction of indigenous people as pure and infallible. From this position, outside critics are easily dismissed as prejudiced people who are protecting their social privileges. I feel that a respectful critique of some of the projects of the indigenous movement may be a sign of respect for indigenous peoples and an indication of understanding indigenous individuals as equals with whom a conversation can be held. This is important because I believe that democratic societies should be based, among other things, in respectful and argumentative conversations, conversations that, one hopes, will start to include everyone—indigenous people, women, people of African descent, and other marginalized sectors of the population—with an equally respected voice. In the same way that I consider it important to criticize some indigenous projects, I am willing to listen to the criticisms of my interlocutors. As a professor in a graduate program for indigenous people from throughout Latin America organized by FLACSO (Facultad Latinoamericana de Ciencias Sociales) [Latin American Faculty for Social Sciences] Ecuador, I have had the opportunity to share my work with indigenous graduate students. I agree with Kay Warren that it is important, although it may not be always easy, to share our work with the societies and groups we study. It is interesting that many of the indigenous students and activists with whom I have shared my work have not been critical but have agreed with my interpretation of their ambivalence toward the reproduction of indigenous culture. The discussion of the occasional conflicts between the preservation of indigenous values and customs and human and women's rights has been more difficult. I see sharing my work with the government officials and intellectuals that I have analyzed in these pages as a more problematic project. This may be because, unlike indigenous people, we are not used to being analyzed academically.

What has been the role of the state and capital in processes of identity formation in a context of increasing globalization? I have shown that the state has not become weaker at an international border or in the context of processes associated with globalization, such as the promotion of commercial agriculture for export, international tourism, or international migration. Mixtec migrants relate to all these processes of globalization; they live in both sides of the Mexico–United States border, they are the preferred labor force in export-oriented agriculture, they seek to profit from international tourism by competing with the middle classes, and they are among the most transnational of indigenous groups. I argue that even when indigenous migrants become more independent because of their transnational connections, the Mexican state has been remarkably effective in influencing their identity. Furthermore, the state has contributed to the construction of identities in ways that fit well with novel global situations: for example, state institutions have reinforced the figure of the "indigenous migrant day laborer" in a context in which export-oriented agriculture has become a central economic sector and has increasingly relied on this kind of worker. From this point of view, institutions of the Mexican state have supported the local and global capital interests that profit from export-oriented agriculture. In chapters 2 and 4 I also show how local authorities favor the interests of the local bourgeoisie, protecting private over public property in San Quintín, and favoring merchants against women vendors in Tijuana. This support is not free from contradictions and tensions, however, as the state through the National Indigenist Institute and the Program in Solidarity with Day Laborers has organized agrarian workers to strike against agrarian capitalists, or through Tijuana's city hall has granted indigenous women permits to sell crafts in public spaces against the interests of local merchants. In addition, different sectors of the bourgeoisie may have different interests that may or not be served by state institutions: whereas agrarian entrepreneurs are interested in promoting the migration of day laborers from the southwest of Mexico and in reinforcing their Indian status, urban merchants claim that their interests are affected by this migration and by the use of this ethnicity to make profits from tourists. In other words, the state has to pick and choose and mediate between different interests and agendas: the contrasting interests of agrarian and urban border entrepreneurs as well as the need to legitimate itself as the advocate for the downtrodden and to get political support from poor sectors of the population.

In the discourses of state officials and other advocates, grassroots migrants are not allowed to choose whether they want to assimilate or to preserve a distinct ethnic identity. Government officials, scholars, and others promote the preservation of the "purity" of indigenous culture as they understand it, sometimes against the will of grassroots indigenous people. The "culture" that many of these advocates sponsor is neither a form of recognition for the Other nor a space for the Other's voice. For instance, according to an official of the Department of Public Education, indigenous culture is not something that grassroots migrants possess, but something that needs to be taught to them by leaders trained by the state. In chapter 4, I show how the approach of scholars who construct manifestations of poverty as indigenous culture contrast with the position of street vendor women, who, for their part, have a more dynamic and less essentialist understanding of their own situation (although on occasion these women use essentialist understandings of themselves for their own purposes). The director of the nongovernmental organization where I worked emphasized the moral, intellectual, and physical differences between indigenous migrants and people like her. Moreover, she thought that it would not be possible or desirable to overcome these differences. Taking into account that the idea of "culture" is an abstraction, a discourse shaped by scholars, government officials, or by some other kind of elite (including indigenous intellectuals), we could speculate whether "culture" is by definition a category always imposed on the grassroots.

The question of the imposition of a certain understanding of culture on migrants is linked to the phenomenon of paternalism, to the idea that Indians are not capable adult citizens able to choose who they want to be and how they want to achieve that being, and that, therefore, somebody else (who means well) should choose for them. Donald Van der Veer (1986) defines paternalism as the interference with the autonomy of another for his or her own good. Van der Veer argues that paternalism is only justified in cases of permanent or temporary incompetence of the recipient of the paternalist act and that it is very problematic when applied to the poor, women, racial minorities, and other vulnerable social groups that are competent to make their own decisions. Because paternalism, despite its

beneficial intentions, assumes the inequality of the recipient party, Mary
Jackman (1994) has defined this as the phenomenon of discrimination
without the expression of hostility. I claim in the introduction and show
throughout this book that paternalism is essential both to an understanding of interethnic relations at the Mexican border, in Latin America, and
elsewhere, and an under-studied phenomenon in anthropology and Latin
American studies.

How does paternalism manifest itself at the Mexican border? Indigenous migrants are often represented as childish, passive, nonrational beings who need to be represented by a mestizo (read "rational") advocate.
Therefore, they are defined as lovable, good-natured, but definitely not
equal to mestizos. In the press debate about the San Quintín riot, Indians
are not portrayed as rational agents able to organize by themselves. Their
actions are blamed either on outside agitators, physical need, or alcohol. In
chapter 3, government agents represent themselves as privileged advocates for indigenous people against agrarian entrepreneurs and other
branches of the government, following a colonial tradition in which the
Crown and the Church were in charge of protecting indigenous communities from exploitative settlers (Wolf 1982). In chapter 4, an anthropologist
argues that he should guide and help those who cannot help themselves. In
chapter 5, the director of a nongovernmental organization treats indigenous migrants, including intellectuals and community leaders, like children, depriving them of the power and respect that comes with age. She
believes that their inadequate intellectual ability sets a limit for development and that they are not capable of understanding what is best for them
and making their own choices.

As noted throughout the text, these different manifestations of paternalism originate in the colonial definition of Indians as nonrational, as opposed to mestizos who were described as *de razón* (rational). Indigenous
people were also considered minors in colonial legislation. Indians could
not represent themselves in legal and other matters and had to be represented by an advocate who came from those groups defined as rational and
typically was a representative of the Crown or the Church. Today state officials, politicians, development workers, and scholars are the typical advocates for indigenous migrants at the Mexican border and elsewhere.
Throughout Latin America, religious groups play a pivotal role as advo-

cates for indigenous peoples. However, at the border, Catholic and Protestant groups have not yet focused specifically on indigenous migrants, because they expect to find mestizos in such a context and because the wave of indigenous migrants from the south is a relatively recent phenomenon.[3]

The representation of non-Western people as childish and passive is not unique to Latin American indigenous peoples. For example, Sherry Ortner (1999a) has noted that Himalayan Sherpas were also represented as childish and passive by the Orientalist discourses of Western mountaineers. Postcolonial scholars inspired by the work of Edward Said (1979) have also documented that non-Western peoples have been represented by Westerners as passive and irrational, whereas only Westerners are constructed as rational agents.

Another important characteristic of paternalism at the border is that exclusion is interpreted as a form of protection for indigenous people, who are excluded "for their own good." A government official claims that indigenous people should be segregated from mestizos in order to be protected from racism. This means that indigenous migrants would be denied access to education and mainstream jobs. The victim, not the victimizer, is punished. Tijuana's merchants "protect" indigenous children from their mothers and indigenous women from an "unrewarding" profession when they ask the local authorities to remove street vendor women from the tourist center, excluding them from their means of livelihood. Scholars claim that indigenous culture, as a representative of the Mexican nation at the border, should be protected from foreign influences coming from religious aid groups and tourists. However, both tourist and North American aid groups are important sources of economic resources for indigenous women. Mestizos are allowed to take advantage of the border economy, whereas indigenous people are not.

Paternalistic discrimination is pervasive at the Mexican border. Indigenous migrants are constructed as lovable inferiors as long as they stay in their proper place as defined by the northern Mexican elites and middle classes. When indigenous migrants enter into economic competition with the middle classes, as in the case of indigenous women street vendors who compete with Tijuana's merchants for tourist business, more hostile stereotypes arise. Indigenous women are represented as outsiders from different social spaces and as deviants from mainstream gender norms, again as

defined by the middle classes. They become undeserving poor whose interests should not be taken into account. Hostile stereotypes are not absent
from the fields of San Quintín, where indigenous day laborers are excluded
from better-paid packing jobs because they are "dirty and too short" to
reach the packing belts. Like urban indigenous women, day laborers are
represented as outsiders, representatives of a transient population that
does not deserve special accommodations. As often happens with manifestations of racism, this phenomenon tends to be denied in northern Mexican society.[4] For northern Mexicans, racism is reflected in the treatment of
Mexican immigrants in the United States. It is interesting that North
American racism is used as a metaphor to talk about internal racism. Racism is located in the past in the discourses of the middle classes. In the
press debate after the 1996 riots in San Quintín, discrimination against indigenous day laborers is portrayed as a legacy of the colonial or Porfirian
past. Those coming from central Mexico see it as a regional phenomenon.
The northern middle classes perceive it as an import from the nation's
south. As Teun Van Dijk (2002, 311) notes, racism is usually elsewhere in the
discourse of elites: "Racism is denied in many ways. First of all, racism is
usually elsewhere: in the past (during slavery or segregation), abroad
(apartheid in South Africa), politically at the far right (racist parties), and
socially at the bottom (poor inner cities, skinheads)."

Sherry Ortner (1999a) has argued that the "orientalist" stereotypes of
those who hold more power are not the whole story. It is important to focus
on how common people accommodate, resist, or work through imposed
identities that have important effects in their lives. In this book, I have
shown that grassroots indigenous migrants sometimes accommodate to
dominant stereotypes or use them strategically for their own purposes. For
example, a day laborer leader in San Quintín accepts representations of
indigenous migrants as passive and innocent, probably to escape repression by the state and employers. A female indigenous street vendor leader
claims that Indians are the real Mexicans in order to claim respect for herself and her followers. In other instances, grassroots migrants forcefully
reject the stereotypes of both their foes and their advocates. Advocates
transform a particular socioeconomic situation in destiny by calling it "culture." Indigenous women street vendors, however, propose a more dynamic understanding of their own identity—one that, whether they

preserve their Mixtec language and identity or not—emphasizes their right and their children's right to have access to education and socioeconomic mobility. Nevertheless, as a perverse consequence of a tradition in which advocates represent the voice of indigenous people to the larger society, these grassroots opinions are rarely heard by the majority. Indigenous voices are ignored unless they replicate what the mainstream society is willing to hear. This is why indigenous leaders sometimes see themselves as being pressured to reproduce essentialist stereotypes. As a Peruvian female indigenous student argued to mestizos criticizing indigenous essentialism in a conference at FLACSO, Ecuador: "If I came here dressed in Western gear and claiming that I am a lower-class mestiza or that my indigenous identity is ambiguous and not pure, would you listen to me or would I even be here to speak?"

I will comment briefly on one central aspect of the methodology of this book: What have we learned from studying up that we would not know otherwise? Why and how should anthropologists study up? What difficulties does the anthropologist encounter when applying this methodology and how can these difficulties be overcome? I show that when we study up we are able to perceive a part of reality that otherwise remains veiled and unexamined.

In many excellent ethnographies of Latin America by North American scholars we get a detailed and rich analysis of indigenous peoples, urban popular groups, and so on. However, most of the time we do not know what are the relationships of the subaltern to more powerful groups in their own societies. How is power deployed? How do the more powerful actors think and act when relating to subalterns and when interacting among themselves? How do the discourses and practices of the powerful fit into longer historical processes and traditions? In many ethnographies of Latin America by North American scholars it seems that only the subaltern and the North American anthropologist exist, leaving out an important part of the social reality of these countries and projecting a particular image of Latin America as homogeneously vulnerable and subordinate in relation to the West.

In scholarship about Latin America written by Latin Americans, these groups are also often left out and remain unexamined, perhaps because these are the groups to which the scholars belong and they may not have either the distance or the will and curiosity to study the powerful. Of course, there are excellent exceptions to this, like the work of Adler Lomnitz and Pérez Lizaur (1987), Adler Lomnitz (2001), Coronil (1997), and others.

There are also reasons for these silences. It is difficult for North American scholars as outsiders from these societies to have access to these more powerful groups, or, perhaps, many scholars do not have an interest in studying subjects with whom they do not feel empathy. For Latin American scholars, it requires courage to research, write, and publish about those in power in societies where academia, politics, and economic groups are not that clearly differentiated and where the boundaries between groups are blurred. Perhaps because I am a Spaniard I had a more advantageous position. In a postcolonial context, as a Spaniard, I was somewhat recognized as an insider who had a definite position to fill in Mexican society. In addition, the status derived from a metropolitan origin facilitated access to elitist, if not elite, subjects. Even indigenous people, who as we have seen have to a certain degree accommodated to postcolonial hierarchies and discourses, are fond of relating to a Spaniard. At the same time, I was an outsider who did not confront the difficulties and consequences of writing about those with a certain amount of influence.

Even with this presumably advantageous position, it was not easy for me to study up. My position helped me get access while doing fieldwork, and I had the additional and obvious advantage of knowing the Spanish language and its subtleties well. However, I had to overcome my shyness and learn to act in particular situations, which is not too different from studying any other group, subaltern or not, to which we do not belong. I am aware that studying up may not be available to every scholar in every situation. In order to have access to those in power the researcher must be at least partially accepted as an equal. This leads to one difficulty of the project: if you are an equal you will be perceived as betraying those you study if you write a critical account. Some scholars who have studied up have solved this difficulty by studying elites in history or through documents in order to avoid personal contact with them. Other scholars, like Penelope Harvey (2002), write about regional elites that may be powerful in a local context but do not have influence at higher national or international levels.

After writing this ethnography, I feel that the writing and publishing stage is the most difficult part of studying up: The anthropologist must be courageous and overcome both real and imaginary fears: for example, the fear of finding in a conference the very people you are writing about, the fear of being harshly criticized by those who are hostile to what you are writing because they feel themselves reflected in it, and so on. Moreover, when you write this kind of ethnography, which will not please everybody, you are burning some bridges. Some scholars have had to change their geographic area of study after writing about subjects with local influence. The anthropologist does pay a price, and I understand very well why, despite Nader's call to study up, there is still, more than three decades later, little written from this point of view. However, in order to understand power and its deployment it is important, if not essential, to study those who exercise it. Parts of social reality that were unexamined and veiled are beginning to be explored. From the point of view of this study three issues that are central to what the book seeks to understand can be examined with this methodology:

- First, the impact of those in power in processes of identity formation. Without this methodology, processes that originate from above could have been interpreted as coming from the bottom up.
- Second, discrimination and prejudices. In order to study them in all their particularities and in very specific contexts, the ethnographic method and the observation of non-Indian subjects who interact with indigenous migrants is adequate.
- Third, paternalism and its concrete deployment at the Mexican border. Perhaps the reason paternalism is an important yet understudied topic is that anthropologists have not studied up enough in Latin America and elsewhere. Perhaps for this very reason some of the best works about paternalism are historical or philosophical, coming from disciplines whose methodology does not require direct contact with those exercising power.

NOTES

INTRODUCTION

1. The Instituto Nacional Indigenista (INI) [National Indigenist Institute], founded in 1948, was the institution that applied state policies in indigenous regions and for indigenous peoples. President Vicente Fox from the Christian Democrat Partido de Acción Nacional (PAN) [National Action Party], elected in 2000, was the first president from an opposition party rather than from the Partido Revolucionario Institucional (PRI) [Revolutionary Institutional Party], which ruled Mexico for nearly seven decades. Fox decided to close INI in 2003 and replace it with the Comisión Nacional para el Desarrollo de los Pueblos Indígenas (CONADEPI) [National Commission for the Development of Indigenous Peoples].

2. After the institutionalization of the Revolution and until recently, Mexican workers were pressured to join official unions linked to the ruling party, PRI. Independent unions started to appear in the last decades of the twentieth century, suffering varying levels of repression.

3. Caso was a prominent Mexican indigenist and the founder of the National Indigenist Institute.

4. As a result of racialized definitions of the nation, in Mexico mixed-blood people, or mestizos, have been defined as the mainstream, unlike the United States, where the mainstream has been understood as white. The Mexican state, influenced by early twentieth century anthropology, has interpreted the differences between mestizos and indigenous people as cultural, although traces or earlier racial discourses have not completely disappeared and what "cultural" means is contested. Boundaries between these categories can vary or be manipulated depending on the context.

5. Interestingly, this indicator does not take into account that indigenous people may marry non-Indians (a phenomenon that is common in Tijuana and San Quintín) who can pass their ethnic identity onto their children or that children of Indians may think of themselves and be identified socially as mestizos after a process of cultural change. Census makers use a cultural argument to justify this indicator: culture is reproduced in the home. However, if one of the parents is mestizo, his or her "culture" could also be passed on to children. Moreover, children who do not speak the mother tongue of their parents and who do not identify as indigenous may prove that indigenous culture has not been passed on to younger generations. Despite the use of culture by census makers, this indicator seems to refer us back to the biological concept of race because it is based on ancestry. We could even argue that it goes beyond race because affines become Indian by association.

6. This phenomenon is not unique to the north of Mexico. As Teun Van Dijk (2002) has argued, it is difficult for any society to officially acknowledge the existence of discrimination. Racism is often displaced to the past, another region, or another social class. In addition, after the Revolution, official discourses have defined Mexico as a nondiscriminatory state. Recent Mexican scholarship is starting to challenge this assumption. See, for example, Hernández Castillo (2001) and Leyva (2003).

CHAPTER 1   MIXTEC COMMUNITIES AT THE MEXICAN BORDER

1. A program in which Mexico and the United States officially organized the temporary migration of Mexican laborers to work in commercial agriculture in the United States from 1942 to 1964.
2. PRONASOL was a government program that started in the early 1990s and used funds from recently privatized state enterprises to target the poorest sectors of the population. Scholars argue that this program helped control social unrest in a period of structural adjustment and build the power of President Salinas de Gortari, who had been accused of electoral fraud in the 1988 elections. See Cornelius, Craig, and Fox (1994).
3. The program was based in the idea of popular participation and organization.
4. Until recently, Mexican workers had to join official unions dependent on the PRI. These unions were accused of being corrupt and sympathetic to employers. Independent unions such as CIOAC were illegal.

CHAPTER 2   THE MAKING OF VULNERABILITIES

1. Nontraditional agro-exports are products such as vegetables, tropical fruits, and flowers that were not exported before the 1970s because they were very perishable. Thanks to improvements in cultivation, packing, and transportation, these delicate items can now be successfully shipped overseas (Thrupp 1995). Nontraditional agro-exports are addressed to an affluent market that seeks healthy foods, exotic flavors, and decorative extras such as flowers. Capital and expertise are needed to produce and ship such delicate items and allocate them to volatile markets. For this reason, small producers are unable to compete unless they receive help from transnational firms or nongovernmental organizations (Thrupp 1995).
2. Export-oriented contract farming of nontraditional agro-exports has become increasingly important in Third World countries in desperate need of foreign exchange. International financial institutions such as the International Monetary Fund and USAID have promoted this kind of agriculture (Dolan 2002; Thrupp 1995; Watts 1992). The north of Mexico was one of the first areas to join this process (Thrupp 1995). In the typical contract, the farmer provides land and labor, and the transnational firm supplies seeds, fertilizers, and technological advice, participates in production decisions, and exports, promotes, and sells the product in developed countries (Dolan 2002; Striffler 2002; Watts 1992). Unlike traditional foreign-owned plantations, contract farming allows transnational companies to avoid such problems as nationalist pressures, local regulations, and expropriations and reduces costs related to the acquisition of land. Contract farming is associated with what is considered a new phase of capitalist development sometimes called "post-Fordism" (in reference to the Ford automobile factory, which first

implemented a system of production based on the assembly line, labor control, large factories, and mass production of standardized items), "flexible capitalism," or "neoliberalism" (see Striffler 2002). Some characteristics of this stage, which according to scholars started in the 1970s, are the shift from direct production to subcontracting (fragmentation of production processes); an emphasis on exports and the globalization of production; and additional segmentation of labor markets characterized by a core of full-time workers who enjoy higher salaries and benefits and a "periphery" of subcontracted, temporary laborers who receive lower salaries and no benefits. This segmentation of labor markets, not surprisingly, tends to take place along racial, ethnic, and gender lines. Although these processes are not new, they have intensified in recent decades. See Harvey (1989) for an interesting discussion of Fordism and post-Fordism.

3. The Mixtec language is spoken in the states of Oaxaca, Guerrero, and Puebla in a mountainous region called La Mixteca.

4. *Enganche* is a traditional way to hire day laborers in Mexico. The agrarian entrepreneur sends an employee familiar with a poor rural area, often a native of the region, to hire workers, arrange their trip north, and often advance them some money. Day laborers hired in this way are tied to a particular patrón for whom they work for the entire harvest season.

5. The Spanish words used in the press are *violencia* (violence) or *revuelta social* (social uprising), depending on the political position of the journalist or newspaper.

6. Ejidos were granted by the Mexican state to peasant communities through the agrarian reform that was implemented after the institutionalization of the 1910 Revolution, particularly during and after the government of President Lázaro Cárdenas (1934–1940). These land grants were believed to replicate pre-Hispanic forms of landownership. "In ejidos land is held communally, farmers are assigned individual lots to cultivate, and each member of the community is supposed to have equal access to pasture lands and other commons" (Nugent 1993, 23).

7. That was before the reform of article 27 of the Mexican constitution in 1992, when ejidos were privatized.

8. Javier Cruz Aguirre, "Los García y los latifundios simulados," *Zeta,* March 26–April 3, 1997, 26A.

9. Andrea Becerril and Jorge Cornejo, "No se porqué se quejan. En su tierra viven peor, dicen patrones," *La Jornada,* July 18, 1996.

10. Day laborers are expected to be paid weekly on Baja Californian ranches.

11. For an analysis of the Chiapas uprising, see Collier and Quaratiello (1994), Nash (2001), Stephen (2002).

12. Some day laborers combine work in San Quintín with work in commercial agriculture in the United States. Others change their earnings into U.S. dollars to avoid currency devaluations.

13. Ethnicity in Mexico, unless otherwise specified, makes reference to Indians. Some emphasis has been put recently into the study of what is called "the third root," Afro-Mexicans, and other ethnic groups, such as Arabs and Jews. However, dominant discourses are still framed in terms of Indian (understood as ethnic) versus mestizo (conceived as mainstream).

14. PRONSJAG started as a branch of Programa Nacional de Solidaridad (PRONASOL), founded by President Carlos Salinas de Gortari (1988–1994). PRONASOL channeled

funds from the privatization of state enterprises and international sources to organized grassroots groups for concrete projects. Grassroots organizations were expected to finance part of the projects with money and/or labor. PRONASOL was also one among a number of programs promoted by international financial organizations, such as the International Monetary Fund, to ease the transition from protectionist state policies to a reduction of the role of the state in social welfare in a number of countries. These programs targeted and co-opted the poorest sectors of the population. PRONSJAG targeted specifically day laborers and worked in the same way as other PRONASOL programs.

15. Although, to avoid conflicts, these institutions eventually divided the day laborer population between themselves. INI ended up working with the settled population, whereas PRONSJAG addressed workers living in employer-provided camps.

16. Becerril and Cornejo, "No se porqué se quejan."

17. Andrea Becerril and Jorge Cornejo, "Ordena el gobierno bajacaliforniano mejorar condiciones de los jornaleros," *La Jornada,* July 20, 1996.

18. Becerril and Cornejo, "No se porqué se quejan."

19. Becerril and Cornejo, "Ordena el gobierno bajacaliforniano."

20. Becerril and Cornejo, "No se porqué se quejan."

21. Ibid.

22. Jorge Cornejo, "Jornaleros ocupan obras de una clínica del seguro social," *La Jornada,* January 19, 1997.

23. Francisco Vargas, "Jornaleros tomaron un hospital del IMSS por incumplimiento de compromiso oficial," *Cambio,* January 18, 1997.

24. After the riots, the Mexican military investigated the following organizations to which day laborers from Santa Anita allegedly belonged: Indigenous Oaxacan Bi-National Front (FIOB); Legal Assistance for Indigenous People (ALIAC); Organization of the Triqui People (OPT; the Triquis are an indigenous group from Oaxaca); Independent Central of Agrarian Workers and Peasants (CIOAC); Movement for the Unification of Independent Day Laborers (MUJI). Other organizations, such as the Confederation of Mexican Workers (CTM) and the Revolutionary Confederation of Workers and Peasants (CROC), to which some workers in Santa Anita belonged, were not investigated because they were official unions (*Zeta,* December 13–19 1996).

25. Pedro Sánchez, Bernardo Peñuelas, and Icíar Gortázar, "Violencia en San Quintín," *Mexicano,* July 5, 1996, 1.

26. Icíar Gortazar, "Más vigilancia en campos agrícolas," *Mexicano,* July 6, 1996, 1.

27. For colonial representations of Indians as minors in legislation and informal practices, see Guerrero (1994), Von Humboldt (1988), and Wolf (1982).

28. Horacio Carvajal, "Violencia Mixteca," *Mexicano,* July 8, 1996.

29. Sergio Anzures, "Explotación y marginación en San Quintín," *La Jornada,* July 5, 1996, 1.

30. Hortensia Martínez and Santiago Flores, "Denuncia CIOAC explotación de mano de obra infantil," *Cambio,* July 7, 1996, 4.

31. Carvajal, "Violencia Mixteca."

32. Icíar Gortazar, "Más vigilancia en campos agrícolas," *Mexicano,* July 6, 1996, 1.

33. Bernardo Peñuelas, "Normalidad en San Quintín. Los trabajadores no somos violentos," *Mexicano,* July 11, 1996, 1.

34. The north of Mexico is constructed, like the frontier myth of the southwestern

United States, as a land of opportunity for self-made men of humble origins and as inherently democratic, in contrast to the hierarchical and aristocratic south. As in the United States, indigenous peoples from the area were excluded from this idea of democracy (León Portilla 1972).

35. Atahualpa Garibay, "Denuncian guardias blancas en San Quintín," *Cambio,* July 6, 1996, 1.

36. Ensenada is the nearest city to San Quintín. Some of San Quintín's farmers live in Ensenada.

37. See Sergio Anzures, "Orígenes de la violencia en el valle de San Quintín," *Mexicano,* July 6, 1996, 1, and Atahualpa Garibay, "Alertan sobre riesgo de conflictos graves en San Quintín," *Cambio,* July 7, 1996, 3.

38. Francisco Vargas, "San Quintín: Olla de presión," *Cambio,* July 7, 1996, 5.

39. Lozoya, "Explotación en San Quintín," *Cambio,* May 4, 1996, 3.

40. Stavenhagen may have a different interpretation today, but his earlier 1970s work is still influential.

41. Andrea Becerril and Jorge Cornejo, "Riesgo de nueva revuelta por las condiciones inhumanas en la zona," *La Jornada,* July 17, 1996.

42. Tonatiuh Guillén, "Moderna injusticia en Baja California," *Cambio,* July 11, 1996, 2.

43. Vargas, "San Quintín."

44. Colloredo-Mansfeld (1998) links ideas of hygiene in the Andes to race instead of culture, because impurity is believed to be inherent to Indian bodies.

45. International human rights and labor organizations are starting to hold transnational companies accountable for the abuses committed by their providers, however (Brysk 2000).

CHAPTER 3   "WE ARE AGAINST THE GOVERNMENT, ALTHOUGH WE ARE THE GOVERNMENT"

1. It is telling that the division of anthropology was located within the Department of Agriculture. That signals that anthropology was associated with Indians and, more specifically, with the problem of how to integrate Indians into the nation. Indians, on their part, were associated with agriculture and the countryside.

2. According to Luis Vázquez León (forthcoming) the National Program in Solidarity with Day Laborers has been characterized by a pro-ethnic approach in other regions of México and has collaborated closely with INI. The situation in Baja California seems to be an exception, explained by the personal philosophy and background of the director at the time.

3. Racism and discrimination are associated at the Mexico–United States border with the treatment of Mexican immigrants in the United States. Interestingly, North American discrimination against Mexicans is used as a metaphor for discussing internal racism.

4. This happened in the context of the reform of article 27 of the Mexican constitution in 1992, which allowed the privatization of ejido lands, and in the context of the Chiapas uprising, which started in January 1994.

CHAPTER 4   THE CULTURE OF EXCLUSION

1. Clothing shops are able to sell North American brands at lower prices because garments are made in Mexico to take advantage of lower wages. Visitors from the

United States, especially the elderly, who need more medicines and tend to have lower incomes, patronize Mexican drugstores, which offer their merchandise at lower prices and without a prescription.

2. There is another section of the city, outside the tourist center, where middle-class Tijuanenses enjoy food and entertainment and where North American tourists are generally not welcome.

3. At least that is what they said when I interviewed them. I have been warned that indigenous women might have thought that I was North American and might have been trying to please me when they praised North Americans. I leave this for the reader to interpret.

4. For colonial representations of Indians as minors who need to be represented by mestizo advocates, see Guerrero (1994), Von Humboldt (1988), and Wolf (1982).

CHAPTER 5   RACE, MATERNALISM, AND COMMUNITY DEVELOPMENT

1. Mixtec women did not wear hats in Tijuana.

2. Nongovernmental organizations (NGOs) have been defined as not-for-profit private organizations that undertake efforts of development and social assistance. They may be funded by the state or by international institutions. In Latin America, the majority of NGOs are of two kinds: religious organizations and research centers (Arellano López and Petras 1994).

3. NGOs typically do not allow their clients to work with other organizations even when these organizations have similar aims.

4. This topic has already been explored in other contexts by Occhipinti (2003), who studied NGO understandings of ethnic identity in the Andes and Chaco region of Argentina, and Bretón (2001), who explored the relationship between NGOs and indigenous organizations in Ecuador.

5. The Salesians targeted poor mestizos with their programs: they required official documents and certificates of elementary education that indigenous migrants rarely had. However, after my suggestion, they accepted a few indigenous migrant women in spite that these women did not fulfill the requirements.

CONCLUSION   CULTURAL DIFFERENCE AND DEMOCRACY

1. For example, I would question the right of indigenous peoples to exercise customary practices that are based on physical or psychological torture and humiliation (for example, lynching), that are not based on respect for the rights of women, or that in any essential way violate universal human rights.

2. For a complete definition of radical democracy see Fraser (1996).

3. I have carried out a study of Catholic missionaries as advocates for indigenous people in Ecuador. See Martínez Novo (2004).

4. Mexican scholars have become interested in studying racism in recent years: See for example Hernández Castillo (2001), Leyva (2003), and Saldívar (2002).

BIBLIOGRAPHY

PERIODICALS

Cambio, Tijuana, Baja California
Excelsior, Mexico - Distrito Federal
El Heraldo, Tijuana, Baja California
La Jornada, Mexico D.F.
Mexicano, Tijuana, Baja California
Zeta, Tijuana, Baja California.

BOOKS, ARTICLES, AND UNPUBLISHED REPORTS

Abramson, D. 1999. "A Critical Look at NGOs and Civil Society as Means to an End in Uzbekistan." *Human Organization* (fall).

Abu-Lughod, L. 1991. "Writing Against Culture." In *Recapturing Anthropology: Working in the Present*, ed. R. Fox, 137–162. Santa Fe, N.M.: School of American Research Press.

Adler Lomnitz, L. 2001. Redes sociales, cultura y poder. Ensayos de antropología latinoamericana. Mexico City: FLACSO y Porrúa.

Adler Lomnitz, L., and M. Pérez Lizaur. 1987. *A Mexican Elite Family 1820–1980. Kinship, Class and Culture*. Princeton, N.J.: Princeton University Press.

Aguirre Beltrán, G. 1967. *Regiones de refugio.* Mexico: INI.

Alonso, A. M. 1995. *Thread of Blood. Colonialism, Revolution and Gender on Mexico's Northern Frontier.* Tucson: University of Arizona Press.

Anderson, B. 1983. *Imagined Communities. Reflections on the Origin and Spread of Nationalism.* New York: Verso.

Appadurai, A. 1990. "Disjuncture and Difference in the Global Cultural Economy." In *Global Culture. Nationalism, Globalization and Modernity*, ed. M. Featherstone. London: Sage.

———. 1996. *Modernity at Large: Cultural Dimensions of Globalization.* Minneapolis: University of Minnesota Press.

Applebaum, N., A. Macpherson, and K. A. Rosemblatt. 2003. *Race and Nation in Modern Latin America.* Chapel Hill: University of North Carolina Press.

Arellano López, S., and J. Petras. 1994. "La ambigua ayuda de las ONGs en Bolivia." *Nueva Sociedad.* 131: 72–87.

Aretxaga, B. 2003. "Maddening States." *Annual Review of Anthropology.* 32:393–410.

Arizpe, L. 1975. *Indígenas en la ciudad de México: El caso de las Marías.* Mexico: SEP.

Asad, T . 1993. *Genealogies of Religion. Discipline and Reasons of Power in Christianity and Islam.* Baltimore: Johns Hopkins University Press.

Babb, F. 1989. *Between Field and Cooking Pot: The Political Economy of Market Women in Peru.* Austin: University of Texas Press.

Barth, F. 1969. *Ethnic Groups and Boundaries.* Middleton: Waveland Press.

Besserer, F. 1997. "La transnacionalización de los oaxacalifornianos: La comunidad transnacional y multicéntrica de San Juan Mixtepec." Paper presented at the XIX Coloquio de Antropología e Historia Regionales, Colegio de Michoacán.

Bonfil Batalla, G. 1990. *México profundo: una civilización negada.* Mexico D.F.: Grijalbo.

Bourdieu, P. 1977. *Outline of a Theory of Practice.* Cambridge: Cambridge University Press.

Bretón, V. 2001. *Cooperación al desarrollo y demandas étnicas en los Andes ecuatorianos.* Quito and Lleida: FLACSO-Ecuador and Universitat de Lleida.

Bringas, N., and J. Carrillo. 1991. *Grupos de visitantes y actividades turísticas en Tijuana.* Tijuana: Colegio de la Frontera Norte.

Brodkin, K. 1998. "Global Capitalism: What's Race Got to Do With It?" *American Ethnologist* 27 (2): 237–256.

Brysk, A. 2000. *From Tribal Village to Global Village. Indian Rights and International Relations in Latin America.* Stanford, Calif.: Stanford University Press.

Butterworth, D. 1975. *Tilatongo: Comunidad Mixteca en transición.* Mexico: INI.

Caso, A. 1980. *La comunidad indígena.* Mexico D.F.: SEP-Diana.

Castañeda, Q. 1997. "On the Correct Training of Indios in the Handicraft Market at Chichén Itzá: Tactics and Tactility of Gender, Class, Race and State." *Journal of Latin American Anthropology* 2 (2): 106–143.

Chan, S. Y. 2000. "Paternalistic Wife? Paternalistic Stranger?" *Social Theory and Practice* 26 (1): 85–102.

Clark, V. 1988. *Los Mixtecos en Tijuana: Sus mujeres, su trabajo y el turismo.* Tijuana: INAH.

Cohen, A. 1981. *The Politics of Elite Culture: Explorations in the Dramaturgy of Power in a Modern African Society.* Berkeley: University of California Press.

Collier, G. 1994. "Peasant Politics and the Mexican State: Indigenous Compliance in Highland Chiapas." In *Race and Ethnicity in Latin America,* ed. Jorge Domínguez. New York: Garland.

Collier, G., and E. Quaratiello. 1994. *Basta! Land and the Zapatista Rebellion in Chiapas.* Oakland, Calif.: Food First Books.

Colloredo-Mansfeld, R. 1998. "'Dirty Indians,' Radical Indígenas, and the Political Economy of Social Difference in Modern Ecuador." *Bulletin of Latin American Research* 17 (2): 185–205.

———. 1999. *The Native Leisure Class. Consumption and Cultural Creativity in the Andes.* Chicago: University of Chicago Press.

Cope, D. 1994. The Limits of Racial Domination: Plebeian Society in Colonial Mexico City 1660–1720. Madison: University of Wisconsin Press.

Cornelius, W., A. Craig, and J. Fox, eds. 1994. *Transforming State-Society Relations in Mexico.* San Diego: Center for U.S.–Mexican Studies.

Cornia, G., R. Jolly, and F. Steward. 1987. Adjustment With a Human Face: Protecting the Vulnerable and Promoting Growth. Oxford: Clarendon Press.

Coronado, I. 1994. "Women and Public Policy: The Social Construction of Mixtecas as a Target Population." Working paper, Colegio de la Frontera Norte, Tijuana, Mexico.

Coronil, F. 1997. *The Magical State: Nature, Money and Modernity in Venezuela.* Chicago: University of Chicago Press.

Corrigan, P., and D. Sayer. 1985. *The Great Arch. English State Formation as Cultural Revolution*. New York: Blackwell.

Craske, N. 1999. *Women and Politics in Latin America*. New Brunswick, N.J.: Rutgers University Press.

Cross, J. 1998. "Co-optation, Competition and Resistance: State and Street Vendors in Mexico City. *Latin American Perspectives* 25 (2): 41–61.

Dawson, A. 1998. "From Models for the Nation to Model Citizens: Indigenismo and the 'Revindication' of the Mexican Indian, 1920–40." *Journal of Latin American Studies* 30: 279–308.

de la Cadena, M. 1995. "'Women Are More Indian': Ethnicity and Gender in a Community Near Cuzco." In *Ethnicity, Markets and Migration in the Andes,* ed. B. Larson and O. Harris, 329–348. Durham, N.C.: Duke University Press.

———. 1996. "The Political Tensions of Representations and Misrepresentations: Intellectuals and Mestizas in Cuzco (1919–1990)." *Journal of Latin American Anthropology* 2 (1): 112–147.

de la Peña, G. 1986. "Poder local, poder regional: perspectivas socioantropológicas. In *Poder local, poder regional,* ed. J. Padua and A. Vanneph. Mexico D.F.: El Colegio de Mexico.

———. 2002. "Social Citizenship, Ethnic Minority Demands, Human Rights and Neoliberal Paradoxes: A Case Study in Western Mexico." In *Multiculturalism in Latin America,* ed. R. Sieder, 129–156. London: Palgrave..

de la Peña, C., and E. Bermejillo. 1995. "Once Divided: Indigenous Peoples in the United States and Mexico Unite Across the Border." *Abya Yala News* 5 (9): 1.

de la Rosa, M. 1987. *La presencia de grupos norteamericanos en Tijuana.* Tijuana: COLEF.

Delpino, N., and L. Pásara. 1991. "El otro actor en la escena: las ONGDs." In *La otra cara de la luna: Nuevos actores sociales en el Peru,* ed. L. Pasara, N. Delpino, R. Valdellano, and A. Zarzar. Buenos Aires: Manantial.

Díaz Polanco, H. 1997. *Indigenous Peoples in Latin America: The Quest for Self-Determination.* Boulder, Colo.: Westview Press.

Dietz, G. 1995. *Teoría y práctica del indigenismo: el caso del fomento a la alfarería en Michoacán.* Quito: Abya Yala.

Dolan, C. 2002. "Gender and Witchcraft in Agrarian Transition: The Case of Kenyan Horticulture." *Development and Change* 33 (4): 659–681.

Dombrowski, K. 2001. *Against Culture: Development, Politics, and Religion in Indian Alaska.* Lincoln: University of Nebraska Press.

Douglas, M. 1966. *Purity and Danger: An Analysis of the Concepts of Pollution and Taboo.* London: Routledge.

Escobar, A. 1995. *Encountering Development: The Making and Unmaking of the Third World.* Princeton, N.J.: Princeton University Press.

Estado de Baja California. 1995. *Programa de desarrollo regional de San Quintín, B.C.*

Essed, P., and D. T. Goldberg. 2002. *Race Critical Theories.* Malden, Mass.: Blackwell.

Feagin, J., and H. Vera. 1995. *White Racism.* New York: Routledge.

Feder Kittay, E., and E. Feder, eds. 2002. *The Subject of Care: Feminist Perspectives on Dependency.* Lanham, Md.: Rowman and Littlefield.

Ferguson, J. 1990. *The Anti-Politics Machine: Development, Depoliticization and Bureaucratic Power in Lesotho.* Cambridge: Cambridge University Press.

Fernández-Kelly, P. 1983. *For We Are Sold, I and My People: Women and Industry in Mexico's Frontier.* Albany: State University of New York Press.

Fischer, E. 1999. "Cultural Logic and Maya Identity: Rethinking Constructivism and Essentialism." *Current Anthropology* 40 (4): 473–499.

Foster, G. 1967. *Tzintzuntzan: Mexican Peasants in a Changing World.* New York: Elsevier.

Fox, J. 1994. "Targeting the Poorest: The Role of the National Indigenous Institute in Mexico's Solidarity Program." In *Transforming State-Society Relations in Mexico,* ed. W. Cornelius, A. Craig, and J. Fox. San Diego: Center for U.S.-Mexican Studies.

Fraser, N. 1996. "Multiculturalism, Antiessentialism and Radical Democracy: A Genealogy of the Current Impasse in Feminist Theory." In *Justice Interruptus: Critical Reflections on the "Post-Socialist" Condition.* New York: Routledge.

Freeman, C. 2000. *High Tech and High Heels in the Global Economy: Women, Work and Pink Collar Identities in the Caribbean.* Durham, N.C.: Duke University Press.

Friedlander, J. 1975. *Being Indian In Hueyapan: A Study in Forced Identity in Contemporary Mexico.* New York: St. Martin's Press.

Garduño, E. 1991. "Mixtecos en Baja California: El caso de San Quintín." *Estudios Fronterizos* 24–25: 87–113.

———. 2003. "The Yumans of Baja California, Mexico: From Invented Communities to Imagined and Invisible Communities." *Journal of Latin American Anthropology* 8 (1).

Garduño, E., E. García, and P. Morán. 1989. *Mixtecos en Baja California: El caso de San Quintín.* Mexicali: Universidad Autónoma de Baja California.

Gideon, J. 1998. "The Politics of Social Service Provision Through NGOs: A Study of Latin America." *Bulletin of Latin American Research* 17 (3): 303–321.

Gill, L. 1997. "Power Lines: The Political Context of Nongovernmental Organization (NGO) Activity in El Alto, Bolivia." *Journal of Latin American Anthropology* 2 (2): 144–169.

Gledhill, J. 2002. "The Powers Behind the Masks: Mexico's Political Class and Social Elites at the End of the Millennium." In *Elite Cultures. Anthropological Perspectives,* ed. C. Shore and S. Nugent. London: Routledge.

Golden, A. 1996. "Baja in Struggle to Preserve a Multitude of Tongues." *San Diego Union Tribune,* December 2.

Gordon, A., and C. Newfield. 1994. "Critical Response: White Philosophy." *Critical Inquirí* 20 (summer): 737–757.

Gramsci, A. 1971. *Selections from the Prison Notebooks.* New York: International Publishers.

Guerrero, Andrés. 1994. "Una imagen ventrílocua: el discurso liberal de la "desgraciada raza indígena" a fines del siglo XIX." In *Imágenes e Imagineros,* ed. B. Muratorio. Quito: FLACSO.

Guillén, Tonatiuh. 1992. *Frontera norte: Una década de política electoral.* Mexico D.F.: El Colegio de Mexico and COLEF.

Harrison, F. 1999. "Introduction: Expanding the Discourse on Race." *American Anthropologist* 100 (3): 609–631.

Harvey, D. 1989. *The Condition of Postmodernity: An Enquiry into the Origins of Cultural Change.* London: Blackwell.

Harvey, P. 2002. "Elites on the Margins: Mestizo Traders in the Northern Peruvian Andes. In *Elite Cultures,* ed. C. Shore and S. Nugent. London: Routledge.

Hernández Castillo, R. A. 2001. "La antropología aplicada al servicio del estado-nación: aculturación e indigenismo en la frontera sur de Mexico." *Journal of Latin American Anthropology* 6 (2): 20–41.

Hewitt de Alcántara, C. 1984. *Anthropological Perspectives on Rural Mexico*. London: Routledge.

Hill, J., and T. Wilson. 2003. "Identity Politics and the Politics of Identities." *Identities* 10 (1): 1–8.

hooks, bell. 1993. "Images of Whiteness in the Black Imagination." In b. hooks, *Black Looks: Race and Representation*. Boston: South End Press.

INEGI. 1990. *La población hablante de lengua indígena en México. XI Censo de Población y Vivienda, 1990*. Mexico D.F.: INEGI.

INI. 1997. *Panorámica general de la problemática de los jornaleros en San Quintín, B.C.*

INI-SEDESOL. 1994. *Instituto Nacional Indigenista, 1989–1994*. Mexico D.F.: INI.

Jackman, M. 1994. *The Velvet Globe: Paternalism and Conflict in Gender, Class and Race Relations*. Berkeley: University of California Press.

Joseph, G., and D. Nugent. 1994. *Everyday Forms of State Formation. Revolution and the Negotiation of Rule in Mexico*. Durham, N.C.: Duke University Press.

Kearney, M. 1988. "Mixtec political consciousness: From passive to active resistance." In *Rural Revolt in Mexico and U.S. Intervention*, ed. D. Nugent, 113–124. San Diego: Center for U.S.–Mexican Studies.

———. 1991. "Borders and Boundaries of State and Self at the End of Empire." *Journal of Historical Sociology* 4 (1): 52–74.

———. 1995. "The Effects of Transnational Culture, Economy and Migration on Mixtec Identity in Oaxacalifornia." In *The Bubbling Cauldron. Race, Ethnicity and the Urban Crisis*, ed. M. Smith and J. Feagin. Minneapolis: University of Minnesota Press.

———. 1996a. *Reconceptualizing the Peasantry. Anthropology in Global Perspective*. Boulder, Colo.: Westview Press.

———. 1996b. "Introduction." *Latin American Perspectives* 89 (23) 2 (spring): 5–16.

Knight, A. 1990. "Racism, Revolution, and Indigenismo: Mexico, 1910–1940." In *The Idea of Race in Latin America 1870–1940*. Austin: University of Texas Press.

———. 1998. "Populism and Neo-populism in Latin America, Especially Mexico." *Journal of Latin American Studies* 30: 223–248.

Kyle, D. 1999. "The Otavalo Trade Diaspora: Social Capital and Transnational Entrepreneurship." *Ethnic and Racial Studies* 22 (2): 422–446.

———. 2000. *Transnational Peasants: Migrations, Networks, and Ethnicity in Andean Ecuador*. Baltimore: Johns Hopkins University Press.

León Portilla, M., ed. 1970. *Historia de la antigua o Baja California by Francisco Xavier Clavijero*. Mexico: Porrúa.

———. 1972. "The Norteño Variety of Mexican Culture: An Ethnohistorical Approach." In *Plural Society in the Southwest*, ed. E. Spicer and R. Thompson. New York: Weatherhead Foundation.

Lestage, F. 1998. "Crecer durante la migración. Socialización e identidad entre los mixtecos de la frontera norte (Tijuana, Baja California)." In *Diversidad étnica y conflicto en América Latina*, ed. R. Barceló and M. Sánchez. Mexico D.F.: Plaza y Valdés.

Lewis, O. 1951. *Life in a Mexican Village: Tepoztlan Reestudied*. Urbana: University of Illinois Press.

Leyva, X. 2003. "Violence raciale, racisme et relations interethniques en contexte de guerre. Un regard sur le Chiapas et un cup d'œil sur le Guatemala." *Ateliers* 26: 171–196.

Macip, Ricardo. 1997. "Politics of Identity and Internal Colonialism in the Sierra Negra of Mexico." Master's thesis, New School for Social Research, New York.

Martínez, Carmen. 2000. "Between Paternalism and Racism: External Agents and the Construction of the Indigenous Migrant at the Mexico–U.S. Border." Ph.D. dissertation, New School for Social Research, New York.

Martínez Novo, Carmen. 2003. "The Culture of Exclusión: Representations of Indigenous Women Street Vendors in Tijuana, Mexico." *Bulletin of Latin American Research* 22 (3): 249–268.

——— 2004. "Los misioneros salesianos y el movimiento indígena de Cotopaxi, 1970–2004." *Ecuador Debate* 63 (December).

Martínez, Oscar. 1988. *Troublesome Border.* Tucson: University of Arizona Press.

Maybury-Lewis, D. 1997. *Indigenous Peoples, Ethnic Groups and the State.* Boston: Allyn and Bacon.

Melhuus, M. 1996. "Power, Value and the Ambiguous Meanings of Gender." In *Machos, Mistresses and Madonnas,* ed. M. Melhuus and K. Stolen, 230–260. New York: Verso.

Michaels, W. B. 1992. "Race into Culture: A Critical Genealogy of Cultural Identity." *Critical Inquirí* 18 (summer): 655–685.

Millán, S., and M. A. Rubio. 1992. "Mixtecos en la frontera norte." Manuscript prepared for INI, Mexico City.

Montiel Aguirre, G. 1995. "El compromiso de servir a nuestros hermanos de raza mixteca." *Comunidad educativa* 7 (2).

Moreno, F. 1988. *La cultura popular en Tijuana: lo que cuentan los mixtecos.* Master's thesis, Colegio de la Frontera Norte, Tijuana.

Muratorio, B. 1991. *The Life and Times of Grandfather Alonso. Culture and History in Upper Amazon.* New Brunswick, N.J.: Rutgers University Press.

Nader, L. 1969. "Up the Anthropologist. Perspectives Gained from Studying Up." In *Reinventing Anthropology,* ed. Dell Hymes. New York: Pantheon.

Nagengast, C., and Michael Kearney. 1990. "Mixtec Ethnicity: Social Identity, Political Consciousness, and Political Activism." *Latin American Research Review* 25 (2): 61–91.

Nash, J. 2001. *Mayan Visions: The Quest for Autonomy in an Age of Globalization.* New York: Routledge.

Nugent, D. 1993. *Spent Cartridges of Revolution: An Anthropological History of Namiquipa, Chihuahua.* Chicago: University of Chicago Press.

Stephen, N. 2002. "Gente Boa: Elites in and of Amazonia." In *Elite Cultures. Anthropological Perspectives,* ed. C. Shore and S. Nugent. London: Routledge.

Oboler, S. 1995. *Ethnic Labels, Latino Lives: Identity and the Politics of Representation in the United States.* Minneapolis: University of Minnesota Press.

Occhipinti, L. 2003. "Mujeres como madres, mujeres como agricultoras: Imágenes, discursos y proyectos de desarrollo." *Ecuador Debate* 59: 123–136.

Omi, M., and H. Winant. 1986. *Racial Formation in the United States.* New York: Routledge.

———. 2002. "Racial Formation." In *Race: Critical Theories,* ed. P. Essed and D. T. Goldberg. Malden, Mass.: Blackwell.

Ortiz, M., and J. Vélez. 1992. "San Quintín, Baja California: El alma en la tierra." *Ojarasca* 13: 32–46.

Ortner, S. 1999a. *Life and Death on Mount Everest.* Princeton, N.J.: Princeton University Press.

——. 1999b. "Thick Resistance: Death and the Cultural Construction of Agency in Himalayan Mountaineering." In *The Fate of Culture: Geertz and Beyond*. Berkeley: University of California Press.

Pérez Ruiz, M. L., and A. Argueta Villamar. 2003. "No todos los indigenismos son iguales (ni tampoco los indigenistas)." *México Indígena* (nueva época) 2 (4).

Poole, D. 1997. *Vision, Race and Modernity: A Visual Economy of the Andean World*. Princeton, N.J.: Princeton University Press.

Proffitt, T. D. 1994. *Tijuana: A Mexican Metropolis*. San Diego, Calif.: San Diego State University Press.

PRONASOL. 1991. *Diagnóstico de las condiciones de vida y trabajo de los jornaleros agrícolas del valle de San Quintín, B.C.* San Quintín: PRONASOL.

Queisser, M., O. Larrañaga, and Panadeiros. 1993. *Adjustment and Social Development in Latin America During the 1980s*. Cologne, Germany: Weltforum Verlag.

Radcliffe, S., and S. Westwood. 1996. *Remaking the Nation: Place, Identity and Politics in Latin America*. London: Routledge.

Redfield, R. 1930. *Tepoztlan: A Mexican Village*. Chicago: University of Chicago Press.

Rénique, G. 2003. "Race, Region and Nation: Sonora's Anti-Chinese Racism and Mexico's Post-Revolutionary Nationalism, 1920s–1930s." In *Race and Nation in Modern Latin America*, ed. N. Applebaum, A. Macpherson, and K. A. Rosemblatt. Chapel Hill: University of North Carolina Press.

Rhett-Mariscal, W. 1998. "Settling In: New Indian Communities and the Transformation of Citizenship in Mexico." Ph.D. dissertation, University of California, San Diego.

Rojas Márquez, E. 1996. "La migración, el camino hacia una nueva identidad." In *Primeras jornadas de radiodifusión indigenista*. Mexico: INI.

Roseberry, W. 1989. *Anthropologies and Histories*. New Brunswick, N.J.: Rutgers University Press.

——. 1994. "Hegemony and the Language of Contention." In *Everyday Forms of State Formation: Revolution and the Negotiation of Rule in Modern Mexico*, ed. G. Joseph and D. Nugent. Durham, N.C.: Duke University Press.

——. 1995. "Introduction." In *Coffee, Society and Power in Latin America*, ed. W. Roseberry, L. Gudmunson, and M. Samper. Baltimore: Johns Hopkins University Press.

Safa, H. 1995. *The Myth of the Male Breadwinner: Women and Industrialization in the Caribbean*. Boulder, Colo.: Westview Press.

Said, E. 1979. *Orientalism*. New York: Random House.

Saldívar, E. 2002. "Everyday Practices of Indigenismo: An Ethnography of Mexico's Instituto Nacional Indigenista." Ph.D. dissertation, New School University, New York.

Sánchez, L. 1994. *Jornaleros indígenas en el noroeste de México*. Mexico D.F.: PRONSJAG.

Sayer, D. 1994. "Everyday Forms of State Formation: Some Dissident Remarks on Hegemony." In *Everyday Forms of State Formation: Revolution and the Negotiation of Rule in Northern Mexico*, ed. G. Joseph and D. Nugent. Durham, N.C.: Duke University Press.

SEP-DGEI. 1996. *Educación indígena alternativa de los grupos étnicos de México*. Mexico: SEP.

Serrano, E., A. Embriz, and P. Fernández. 2002. *Indicadores Socioeconómicos de los pueblos indígenas de México, 2002*. Mexico: INI-CONAPO-UNDP.

Shore, C., and S. Nugent. 2002. *Elite Cultures. Anthropological Perspectives.* London: Routledge.

Sieder, R. 2002. *Multiculturalism in Latin America. Indigenous Rights, Diversity and Democracy.* London: Palgrave.

Sklair, L. 1993. *Assembling for Development. The Maquila Industry in Mexico and the United States.* San Diego, Calif.: Center for U.S.–Mexican Studies.

Smith, R. 1996. "Mexicans in New York: Membership and Incorporation in a New Immigrant Community." In *Latinos in New York: Communities in Transition,* ed. G. Haslip-Viera and S. Baver. Notre Dame, Ind.: University of Notre Dame Press.

Solís Domínguez, D. 1998. "Protestantismo y sociedad en la Frontera Norte: procesos de pluralidad religiosa en la ciudad de Tijuana." Master's thesis, COLEF, Tijuana.

Stabb, M. S. 1959. "Indigenism and Racism in Mexican Thought: 1857–1911." *Journal of Inter-American Studies.* 1: 405–423.

Stavenhagen, R. 1970. "Classes, Colonialism and Acculturation." In *Masses in Latin America,* ed. I. Horowitz. New York: Oxford University Press.

———. 1994. "Challenging the Nation State in Latin America." In *Race and Ethnicity in Latin America,* ed. Jorge Domínguez. New York: Garland.

———. 2002. "Indigenous Peoples and the State in Latin America: An Ongoing Debate." In *Multiculturalism in Latin America,* ed. Rachel Sieder, 24–44. London: Palgrave.

Stepan, N. 1991. *The Hour of Eugenics: Race, Gender and Nation in Latin America.* Ithaca, N.Y.: Cornell University Press.

Stephen, L. 1991. *Zapotec Women.* Austin: University of Texas Press.

———. 1996. "The Creation and Re-creation of Ethnicity: Lessons from the Zapotec and Mixtec of Oaxaca. *Latin American Perspectives* 89 (23): 17–37.

———. 1997. "The Zapatista Opening: The Movement for Indigenous Autonomy and State Discourses on Indigenous Rights in Mexico." *Journal of Latin American Anthropology* 2 (2): 2–41.

———. 2001. "Fighting the Construction of Illegal Aliens: PCUN and Cultural Citizenship for Oregon Farm Workers." Paper delivered at the 2001 meeting of the Latin American Studies Association, Washington DC.

———. 2002. *Zapata Lives! Histories and Cultural Politics in Southern Mexico.* Berkeley: University of California Press.

Stoler, A. 1997. "Carnal Knowledge and Imperial Power: Gender, Race and Morality in Colonial Asia." In *The Gender Sexuality Reader,* ed. R. Lancaster and M. di Leonardo. London: Routledge.

Striffler, S. 1998. "Wedded to Work: Class Struggles and Gendered Identities in the Restructuring of the Ecuadorian Banana Industry." *Identities: Global Studies in Culture and Power* 6 (1).

———. 2002. *In the Shadows of State and Capital: The United Fruit Company, Popular Struggle and Agrarian Restructuring in Ecuador, 1900–1995.* Durham, N.C.: Duke University Press.

Thrupp, L. A. 1995. "Feeding the Global Supermarket." In *Free Trade and Economic Restructuring in Latin America,* ed. F. Rosen and D. McFadyen. New York: Monthly Review Press.

Tilly, Louise, and Joan Scott. 1978. *Women, Work and Family.* New York: Holt, Rinehart, and Winston.

Uphoff, N. 1993. "Grassroots Organizations and NGOs in Rural Development: Opportunities With Diminishing States and Expanding Markets." *World Development* 21 (4): 607–622.

Urban, G., and J. Sherzer. 1992. *Nation States and Indians in Latin America*. Austin: University of Texas Press.

Van Cott, D. L. 1994. *Indigenous Peoples and Democracy in Latin America*. New York: St. Martin's Press.

———. 2000. "A Political Analysis of Legal Pluralism in Bolivia and Colombia." *Journal of Latin American Studies* 32: 207–234.

———. 2002. "Constitutional Reforms in the Andes: Redefining Indigenous-State Relations." In *Multiculturalism in Latin America*, ed. Rachel Sieder, 45–73. London: Palgrave.

Van der Berghe, P. 1967. *Race and Racism. A Comparative Perspective*. New York: John Wiley.

Van der Veer, D. 1986. *Paternalistic Intervention. The Moral Bounds on Benevolence*. Princeton, N.J.: Princeton University Press.

Van Dijk, T. 2002. "Denying Racism: Elite Discourse and Racism." In *Race: Critical Theories*, ed. P. Essed and D. T. Goldberg. Malden, Mass: Blackwell.

Varese, S. 1996. "The Ethnopolitics of Indian Resistance in Latin America." *Latin American Perspectives* 89 (23) 2: 57–71.

Vázquez León, L. 2003. "De identidades numeradas, racionalidades divergentes y la etnicidad entre los jornaleros agrícolas indígenas en el Occidente de Mexico." Paper presented in V Coloquio de Occidentalistas, Universidad de Guadalajara.

———. Forthcoming. "La prevalencia étnica bajo el fin del indigenismo y la nueva proletarización de la población indígena." In L. Vázquez León, *Purepecheo revisitado. Ensayos de inclusión y exclusión étnicas en Michoacán*.

Velasco, L. 1995. "Migración femenina y estrategias de sobrevivencia de la unidad doméstica: un caso de estudio de mujeres mixtecas en Tijuana." In *Mujeres, migración y maquila en la frontera norte*, ed. S. González, O. Ruíz, L. Velasco, and O. Woo. Tijuana: COLEF-COLMEX.

———. 1999. *Comunidades transnacionales y conciencia étnica: Indígenas migrantes en la frontera México-Estados Unidos*. Ph.D. dissertation, El Colegio de Mexico, Mexico City.

———. 2002. *El regreso de la comunidad: migración indígena y agentes étnicos. Los mixtecos en la frontera México-Estados Unidos*. Tijuana: Colegio de Mexico/ Colegio de la Frontera Norte.

Villa Rojas, A. 1955. *Los Mazatecos*. Mexico: Memorias del INI.

Visweswaran, K. 1998. "Race and the Culture of Anthropology." *American Anthropologist* 100 (1): 70–83.

Von Humboldt, A. 1988. *Political Essay on the Kingdom of New Spain*, ed. M. Naples Dunn. Norman: University of Oklahoma Press.

Wade, Peter. 1997. *Race and Ethnicity in Latin America*. Chicago: Pluto Press.

———. 1998. "The Cultural Politics of Blackness in Colombia." In *Blackness in Latin America and the Caribbean,* ed. N. Whitten and A. Torres, 311–334. Bloomington: Indiana University Press.

Warren, K. 1998. *Indigenous Movements and their Critics: Pan-Maya Activism in Guatemala*. Princeton, N.J.: Princeton University Press.

Warren, Kay, and Jean Jackson. 2002. *Indigenous Movements, Self-Representation, and the State in Latin America*. Austin: University of Texas Press.

Watts, M. 1992. "Living Under Contract: Work, Production Politics, and the Manufacture of Discontent in a Peasant Society." In *Reworking Modernity: Capitalisms and Symbolic Discontent,* ed M. Watts and A. Pred. New Brunswick, N.J.: Rutgers University Press.

Weiner, M. 1986. "The Intersection of Race and Gender: The Antebellum Plantation Mistress and her Slaves." *Humboldt Journal of Social Relations* 131 (1 and 2): 374–386.

Whisnant, D. 1983. *All That Is Native and Fine.* Chapel Hill: University of North Carolina Press.

Wingerd, M. 1996. "Rethinking Paternalism: Power and Parochialism in a Southern Mill Village. *The Journal of American History* 83 (3): 872–902.

Wolf, E. 1982. *Europe and the People Without History.* Berkeley: University of California Press.

Young, E. 1994. "The Impact of IRCA on Settlement Patterns Among Mixtec Migrants in Tijuana, Mexico." *Journal of Borderland Studies* 9 (2).

Zamosc, L. 1994. "Agrarian Protest and the Indian Movement in the Ecuadorian Highlands." *Latin American Research Review* 29 (3): 37–68.

INDEX

ABOUT THE AUTHOR

Carmen Martínez Novo is professor and researcher in the anthropology program at Facultad Latinoamericana de Ciencias Sociales Sede Ecuador. Before that, she was assistant professor in the department of sociology and anthropology at Northeastern University, Boston. She has a Ph.D. from the New School for Social Research (now New School University) and has held predoctoral and postdoctoral grants from the Wenner-Gren Foundation for Anthropological Research and the MacArthur Foundation. She is the author of several articles on ethnic identity at the Mexico–U.S. border and is currently doing and publishing research on the indigenous movement in Ecuador.